From Colmar to Kabul

A Journey from Tragedy to Hope

Ariane Geiger Hiriart

Translated into English by:
Dionne Wilson

Le Pélican
Le Pélican USA
www.lepelican.org

Contents

This book is dedicated to my son, Frantz, who was my light and joy during his short stay on earth. His death triggered a spiritual quest that sowed in me the seeds of eternal life.

It is also dedicated to Jacques, my husband, whose trust and encouragement pushed me to write of the experiences that transformed and gave authentic value to our existence. During our thirty-nine years together, he was not only a companion and faithful team leader but much more: he was the love of my life.

I dedicate this to all my guardian angels—they know who they are. And of course, I dedicate this to God, as I hope what I have written here reveals an infinitesimal part of the absolute love He has for us.

Having said this, he spit on the ground, made some mud with the saliva, and put it on the man's eyes. "Go," he told him, "wash in the Pool of Siloam." So the man went and washed and came home seeing. His neighbors and those who had formerly seen him begging asked, "Isn't this the same man who used to sit and beg?" Some claimed that he was. Others said, "No, he only looks like him." But he himself insisted, "I am the man." "How then were your eyes opened?" they demanded. He replied, "The man they call Jesus made some mud and put it on my eyes. He told me to go to Siloam and wash. So I went and washed, and then I could see." "Where is this man?" they asked him. "I don't know," he said.

John 9:6-12

Part One: The Beginning

Chapter One

The Flight of Angels

T he small red-and-white Cessna from the Colmar flying club slowly descended on a sunny afternoon in May 1974. I was twenty-six years old. The pilot had been dropping his share of crazy skydivers all day! I was part of the last group and was about to do my fifth "required" jump. This time the instructor, satisfied with my progress, authorized me to make my dream come true: to jump without the automatic opening strap. I listened conscientiously to his advice: "Ariane, don't rush to pull the handle. We're going to go up 1,200 meters so you will have plenty of time. Arch yourself well to stabilize yourself in the air, lift your head and look at the plane, then slowly count three seconds and pull the handle. If all goes well, I'll drop you at five seconds next time."

Wow! For me, it was the greatest! I was exhausted from the day of training, but excited about the sport I loved so much and which was eating up all my savings.

So I jumped and got out of the plane with no problem. I arched my back, stretched out my arms, raised my head, and looked up at my monitor who was grinning from ear to ear. I was a diligent student, so I slowly counted the seconds: 001, 002, 003, just as I had been taught. I brought both arms forward and with my right hand, as I had been instructed, grabbed the handle of the parachute and pulled it. But unlike the four morning jumps with a dummy grip, nothing happened!

My handle did not move, my parachute remained firmly closed! I fell into the void and could no longer stabilize myself. I turned like a disjointed puppet and watched the earth, the sky, the earth, the sky, on a loop!

Terrified, I understood that I was falling at a rate of about 200 kilometers per hour and the ground was approaching me at breakneck speed. I was terrified and panicking. I saw the green of the terrain and the beige of the earth mixing together. The thought that I was going to crash sent shivers of fear down my spine. I was distraught, I was going down so fast! The earth sucked me in, and I knew it would swallow me up soon. I was perfectly aware of my impending death; it was inevitable. Yet I was still struggling to try something…I felt so stupid!

I finally thought of my reserve parachute stuck to my stomach. It would to save me, I was sure of it. I pulled the handle, but again, nothing happened! I was sure at that moment that I was going to die, because it was too late, I had wasted too much time. I was now about 400 meters from the ground. I knew that if my hitch did not open immediately, I would crash! The canopy of the parachute would not have enough distance to deploy. I saw the details of the grass on the airstrip, the footprints on the dirt road. Everything became enormous and monstrous.

With the energy of despair, I violently pulled on the handle of the ventral again, understanding this was my last chance. The ground was only a few meters away. The air carried me; I was facing the sky where my gaze was lost.

Finally, after several attempts, the handle released! The saving sail burst before my eyes. I was hanging from my reserve parachute. The wind pushed me towards the Timken factory in the industrial area of Colmar. With horror, I realized that, swept away by an eastern wind, I was headed straight towards a large, billowing smokestack! A maddening fear seized me! I grabbed the lines from my stomach and pulled with all my might to get away from the burning crater. My parachute, by paradoxically opening so late, allowed me to be low enough to avoid it, and saved me from being incinerated.

Suddenly I heard a strange noise: it was my head, protected by my metal helmet, echoing as it banged on the first roof where I had landed on my back. I was not in control of anything, I let go and closed my eyes. The second building was so close to the other that I rolled over onto this second roof without even realizing it. Finally, the parachute canopy caught on a small ventilation duct and stopped my fall. I found myself hanging, upright, ten centimeters above the ground in the factory yard.

My friends from the parachute club, who had followed the whole scene, thought they would find me dead. An instructor jumped into his car and rushed over. When he found me, I believe he was close to having a heart attack; he was overcome and could not speak. It was "a lucky break" or for some, "a real miracle." At the time, I didn't believe in God or the devil. I was just glad to be alive-that was all.

Jacques, one of the club members who was nothing special to me at the time, later admitted to saying: "That would have been a shame because I hadn't hit on her yet!"

Many years have passed since that momentous and terrifying experience. If I didn't have the inclination to turn to God and thank him for keeping me alive at the time, today I know that his will was that I would not die on that May 13, 1974. So, I imagine an angel slicing through space at a speed far greater than light, making its way between galaxies to reach me as I was falling to a certain death. Nothing stands in the way of imagining that a slender finger, coated in stardust, blew open the obstinate grip and released the canopy of my reserve parachute. This messenger of the Lord saved my life, by order of the Most High, just in time.

Chapter Two

Free Fall

I have been confronted with death as far back as I can remember. The first was that of my father. He was an Alsatian industrialist whose factory, located in Ingersheim, near Colmar, manufactured cardboard tubes which, when treated, could support the weight of one hundred kilos without breaking. I remember the games of hide-and-seek when, as little children, my sister, my friends, and I would go out to the wooden hut where rolls of paper, boxes of tubes and bags of dust from the paper cutting were stored. We often found multicolored powder in our ears and in the bathwater, little rainbow lumps, clues to our forays into forbidden places.

I remember the smell of Bakelite (synthetic plastic), glue, and resin which was in the air throughout my childhood, the noise of machines, the regular clicking of presses, and the howls of sirens. It was the time when industrialists lived their last days of glory. A few years later, cardboard mills, tube mills, and spinning mills would close one after another, in Alsace, in the North and in the Vosges, victims of the entry of Asian products into the market at unbeatable prices.

I was six-and-a-half years old when my father, who had long been ill, died. The asthma attack that occurred on the evening of December 31, 1953, was fatal. For part of the night, my sister and I heard strange comings and goings in the hallway. I saw a nun's white cornet pass by my bedroom and noticed some unusual noises and a whole different atmosphere. I knew something had happened, and that the routine of our ordinary lives would never return.

In the early hours of the morning, my mother found us in the room where we had been asked to sleep, a room at the end of the corridor where the parquet floor creaked. She gathered us in her arms as her mouth twisted with a sob that she could not suppress, and she told us our father had died. Her blue eyes, bathed in tears, gave her woeful face a theatrical beauty. I can still hear her voice, choked by words too hard for a mom to say, and too sad for a six and nine-year-old to hear. I had a hard time understanding this simple sentence, which determined my future and would upset my whole life's structure, "Daddy is in heaven…Daddy is in heaven, my little girls…"

At that time, the word "death" was not spoken in front of children. No explanations were given and no questions were addressed. It was all cloaked in silence.

I believe we were offered a chance to see him, and we did. The only thing I remember is that this man who was my father was lying on the living room sofa dressed in a dark suit. I remember kissing a white, waxy, already icy cheek. I was sad, but the deep pain and heartbreak came long after.

The shock of his death and his sudden physical disappearance, caused a trauma that has long disturbed my psyche. The ghost of my father often haunted the landscape of my childhood. I did not believe in his death for many years and looked everywhere for him. I thought I recognized him on the street one day and told my mother, who replied that it was not possible. I was unable to grasp the harshness of this reality, and then took refuge in dreams by building a world where I found him. Even after seven years, I stubbornly rejected his departure, which I saw as an abandonment, a lie, or both at the same time.

His death was followed by the drama of the Orleansville earthquake, in which my uncle and aunt perished, leaving my cousin an orphan. Losing his son and daughter-in-law in such an atrocious way caused my grandfather, General Albert Durand's health to decline, and he died six months later, in May 1955.

Disturbed by all these deaths, I was sent to join my sister at a Catholic boarding school in the Alps. There I was, I believe, the youngest of around three hundred girls. I was extremely unhappy there, unable to accept having been uprooted and set down in a hostile environment. I did everything I could to get myself sent home. The bedwetting caused by the death of my father increased even more, my tears redoubled, and I tried everything I could think of to make myself sick—walking in the snow barefoot in my nightgown in 5-degree weather, drinking ink, swallowing strong liquid glue. But I only managed to get a bad cold and a stomach infection which kept me from speaking and eating for two weeks.

Traumatized and starved for love, I felt neglected by the good sisters who were unable to provide the tenderness and compassion that I so badly needed. Being forced to attend Mass every morning, to go to the chapel in the afternoon, to recite obligatory prayers on all kinds of occasions, and then to discover that neither the nuns nor the lay teachers in my classes seemed to apply the gospel, turned me off to any form of religion. So I escaped through dreams, thinking that one day I would get rid of all these lies and be free. For the first time in my life, I wanted to die.

We would go skiing every Thursday, an obligation that I hated because I was very cold for hours. The metal bindings of my heavy wooden skis, painfully embedded themselves in the skin of my shoulders as I walked. I often stopped on a bridge and watched the water rushing about twenty meters below and imagined throwing myself in. Or I hoped a car would stop and take me far away. Frozen tears stuck my eyelashes together. My despair was total.

In the evening, before going to sleep, I begged my Daddy to come and get me. I was ashamed of the bedwetting which was causing me embarrassment with my roommates who had noticed it. I wiped the floor and rinsed my sheets in the early hours of the morning while the girls giggled behind my back. I was transferred to another dorm, without explanation or help. The nuns were necessarily aware, but nothing changed. Many of the boarders seemed unwell, but I felt like I was the most lost and the most unhappy. I still feel the humiliation and loneliness of those days today.

I have no good memories of the boarding school in Saint-Gervais where I spent nearly three years, the saddest of my young existence. In skiing, I only enjoyed the moment when the instructor held me against him in the ski lifts because I was the smallest of the group. This was the only real human warmth I encountered at that time.

Today, during serious events, vulnerable people have access to psychological help and appropriate medications. In the 1950s, on the other hand, no assistance was provided in the event of a crisis. Madame Dolto, a French child-rearing psychologist, was not read at the time. My mother didn't do anything to help. She only sensed my dismay since the boarding school most likely did not alert her. So, I became a dangerous little savage, with strange reactions.

These difficult times favored my intellectual disengagement because I had no desire to learn. Instead, I spent my classes daydreaming. I heard the teachers' reflections through the haze: "It's the little one who's always on the moon, we have the impression that she is in another world, like in a bubble... She dreams all the time."

Boris Cyrulnik, the famous neuropsychiatrist says, "A child who grows up with a mother and father who love each other, has his own little room, and supervised homework, will necessarily have good grades. Grades are not a reflection of intelligence, but a mirror of emotional stability."

Unquestionably, I had none.

My life in Catholic boarding schools was catastrophic in many ways, as I was shuffled to different schools. I became so fed-up at the third institution that the idea of taking my own life began to materialize around the age of twelve. Did I really want to die? I wanted all of this to stop and I was calling out for help. I was suffocating in the confined, limited, dark, and sad world at this new Alsatian boarding school. The Masses, the vespers, the prayers, the punishments, the sacrifices, Lent, and all the superficial religious fervor totally put me off. I felt no freedom to think. It was all ridiculous superstitions to me. We were banned from even walking in the courtyard in pairs for fear of illicit friendships! The letters we sent and received were opened and censored by the nuns. My need for justice and freedom could not tolerate such behavior. My heart was hardening more every day as a revolt brewed inside me.

I also observed the difference in attitude between nuns called *mothers* and those called *sisters*. The first, supposedly representing the intellectuals, taught us lessons and took care of our education. The sisters were relegated to manual work. This distribution of tasks would have been perfectly acceptable without the disdain and derogatory treatment by the *superiors*, which seemed undeserved and uncharitable. Praying so much, these people should have acted differently. The crucifixes around their necks, the rosaries hanging from their waists, the pleated cornets surrounding their faces all represented a religion that I abhorred. The most difficult thing to bear was their harshness and severity. You would have thought that life was all burdens, bitterness, and boredom. Very strict with themselves, they were even more so with all of us. It seemed to me that they could never succumb to the temptation of friendly casualness, to the weakness of a suspended punishment, or to any long-buried tenderness, and all in order to gain a place in paradise.

God had to be different, God had to be somewhere else. My contained rebellion grew into a less and less hidden revolt. I pitifully craved air, lightness, gentleness, and laughter in that suffocating atmosphere. I lacked everything that made life worth living at twelve years old. After more than a year at that boarding school, I decided to end it all. On a weekend at home, I stole a bottle of sleeping pills from my mother's medicine cabinet.

On Monday morning, I swallowed all the pills just before entering the classroom. I felt groggy very quickly and fell face-first on the desk. General panic ensued. The doctor who was called gave me a shot to support my heart and slapped me hard to wake me up. I vomited and was put to bed and slept for twenty-four hours. That was it. The incident was over. I was not dead; there was no scandal. No one wondered about the deeper meaning of my gesture, about the suicidal behavior of a pre-teen, about her distressed cry for help and her need to be heard. None of these women, religious to the core, had enough compassion to talk with me, nor to talk about me. Silence was their only answer, indifference too. Had my mother even been informed? I don't think so since we never talked about it.

I had seen in death a liberating impulse, a salvation in a way. To this day, I don't know if I actually wanted to die. What I do know is that I wanted to run away, one way or another. Like in the Alps on that bridge, I had only one desire: to stop this slow-moving life, this bland and tasteless life, this non-life, that couldn't be satisfied with the little moments of happiness when I was at home in Ingersheim. In fact, this failed suicide attempt triggered in me an understanding of the very real fact that no one would come to my aid no matter what I did. Certainly, at my age I couldn't run my life, I could only obey adults. However, my reasoning was up to me, and no one could tell me what to think.

Later, the experience of those miserable years in boarding school came back to me often. The actions of the men and women of God had been so contrary to what I knew about Jesus, that I started a total break with everything that so much as touched on religion. The idea of a God resembling theirs was unbearable to me and the representation that I had been given until then was unacceptable. Still too young and too inexperienced, I did not understand that God is beyond all religiosity, that He is different, and even entirely *Other*. He had to be looked for elsewhere, deep in one's heart, instead of stupidly throwing everything away. As my friend Henriette told me later in her strong Burgundy accent: "My little Arrrrriane, you threw out the baby with the bath water!"

Yes, I threw it all away, I dumped all forms of spirituality. I went to war as others go on a crusade. I hated the Catholic religion so much that I could no longer visit a church without gagging. I didn't share this hate with anyone, but it was there, deep inside me, inspiring all kinds of bad thoughts. I was not one for half-measures!

Yet, how can I forget that day when, still very young, kneeling in a chapel, I had spoken to the Lord and felt an overwhelming sweetness, a feeling of fullness, and freedom too. Contact with Jesus had nothing to do with the gross parody of humans, this caricature of a God who constantly punishes, or with the sentimentality of a religion that I thought was weak and ridiculous. This was the religion that grown-ups had hitherto shown and taught me. I was looking for something else and especially for the Other. I was confused, but was still discerning Him; I unconsciously sensed His existence.

In that dimly lit chapel, under the gaze of gentle Mary and the benevolent smiles of Saint Joseph, I had made a declaration of love to Jesus with all my child's heart. With clumsy words, I had responded to divine love. I remember the pungent smell of incense and the student right in front of me, also on her knees. Had she also confided in the Lord? After she left, I let the presence of God come over me. I prayed without restraint as only children can. I rushed to Him: "I love you, Lord Jesus, I give you my heart, I would like to do something for you."

I remember the peace and quiet of that chapel. I wanted to stay there for a long time, in the sweetness of the evening. Time did not count anymore; I was frozen in place. Unfortunately, the ringing bells that regulated our lives as students clanged, shrill and unwelcome. Later, in the icy dormitory, I hugged a small hot water bottle filled with lukewarm water and wept over a time gone forever and a colorless future.

If I could, I would gladly sweep away the sadness, injustice, anguish, and lack of love of those difficult years. I would only keep the face-to-face encounter with Jesus--heart-to-heart.

Despite everything, however, I was obliged to make my solemn communion. My heart that day exploded with rage. I felt like a hypocrite since I no longer believed this man-made religion could save me. So what were these vows that I was being asked to renew when they had already been imposed on me in First Communion? Confirm a faith that had been stuck to my forehead during my baptism, when I was barely wailing? It all seemed utterly ridiculous, even dishonest, and inspired disgust and rebellion in me. As Georges Brassens puts it so well, "People don't like to follow any road but their own." Definitely, no, I couldn't walk the shallow path that was offered to me.

During the preparation for this big day, shocked that I did not have a Christian first name, the parish priest and the nuns declared that for the occasion, my name would be Francesca: "The names of the communicants must be chanted in Latin, Ariane, and since your first name does not correspond to a saint, you will be Francesca. Do not forget to come forward when you hear it."   I had it all wrong, I was always the one with the problem. Now, in addition to the rest, the nuns also stole my first name! That made me want to run away even more. So I kicked God out for good, as much as one can at the age of thirteen. Yes, on the day of my solemn communion, I said no to God, forever. At least, that's what I thought…

Chapter Three

Love is in the Air

After a troubled adolescence, I became a liberated young woman, with an ever-rebellious and anti-conventional character, and with a need for love that was never met. I finished my studies in Paris where, adventurous at heart, I discovered skydiving and made my first jump at La Ferté Gaucher. Having found work back in Alsace, I took the opportunity to practice my new passion there, until that unfortunate fall which could have been fatal to me. But that event brought me closer to the tall, nonchalant young man with the surfer look, Jacques.

I don't know what attracted me most to him. Was it his relaxed attitude, his nonconformity, his sense of humor, his dazzling smile, or his immense desire for extreme experiences? Was it because he looked like Rock Hudson and I wanted to feel like the heroine of a romantic movie? Or more simply, was it because his soft gaze melted me and I didn't want to resist him? It was not really what is usually called love at first sight, but rather a quiet and reciprocal observation, a calm attraction based on common tastes and similar character traits. Independent and free spirits, neither of us put up with hypocrisy or convention. We were on the same page, and I was excited to have found a young man as crazy as me.

It was only in sports that we were different. For Jacques, skydiving was the conquering passion . His composure, will, professionalism, and endurance allowed him to climb the skydiving podium on several occasions.

For me, on the other hand, this sport was just an exhilarating game that gave everyone the opportunity to overcome their fear, facing the unnatural act of throwing themselves out of a plane and into the abyss of the sky. It also helped me to learn how to better manage my emotions.

After the serious incident of landing on the factory roof with my stomach in a knot, it was very difficult to jump again. But Jacques always encouraged me to go again with a smile and a wave.

Finally, one day…I broke down.

It was a very early morning. Jacques acted as an instructor because he had the qualifications. We were both in the parachute folding room and I asked him to give me a parachute since I was scheduled on the first plane at 7:30 a.m. When he handed it to me, he kept his hand on mine for a while and looked at me tenderly as he said with barely contained emotion: "Don't worry, everything will be fine; I have chosen your parachute, it will open."

The plane soared in the Alsatian sky for half an hour to reach the planned 3,000 meters. During this ascent we admired the beauty of the landscape below: the blue of the Vosges Mountains, intensified by the April sun, surpassing, if possible, the deep richness of Van Gogh's colors. I will always remember that flight, and especially that jump. It changed my destiny and that of the one who would become my companion for thirty-nine years.

Jacques asked me to stay last on the plane and jump at his signal, which I did. I was no longer a free-fall neophyte and, now free of all anxiety, I enjoyed letting myself be carried by the air like a bird. Then, with a big smile, he approached me and, taking my wrists, drew me to him. That was the first time I experienced that trick, which normally requires serious preparation as the free fall approach is very delicate. But Jacques knew the maneuver and how to pull it off safely, so for me, it was a wonderful surprise!

As we hovered over the terrain below, as if outside of time, he signaled to me that it was time to pull the handle. Pulling me closer he kissed me on the lips, then let go, and disappeared into the sky. I was, literally and figuratively, on a small cloud that only the shock of the opening of my parachute could topple me from. Eyes full of stars and a capsized heart, I landed abruptly, wondering, like a schoolgirl, if I had been dreaming.

This tall and handsome boy, the idol of all the girls, this skydiver with over 4,000 jumps, this impressively built man was undoubtedly too shy to express on terra firma the love he had for me. His statement, with only the sky and the clouds as witnesses, reflected his reserved, modest, and kind character. Later, I would understand that he was also strong-willed yet loving, adventurous but hardworking, and that these personality traits provided the compass for his life. His endearing personality won me over immediately. His demeanor was honest, without pretense or affectation. I fell in love with Jacques and have never regretted it.

At the end of 1975, after a year of living together, we wanted to formalize our love. It was time for Jacques to find a serious job, to think about our future, and to give up his bohemian lifestyle, which had appealed to me so much. Although he had already won fourth place at the French national skydiving championships, he now gave up the dream of becoming a skydiving champion. He was soon hired by a French oil company and sent immediately to a physically demanding job on an oil platform in the North Sea. On one of his returns to Colmar, we got married.

Like me, Jacques had been disappointed with the Catholic church and had abandoned it at the age of fifteen. But despite these feelings, we got married in a church so as not to hurt our families. But we explained to the priest, my mother's distant cousin, that we did not believe in the church's lies and that we would not take communion. This man of faith, filled with the Holy Spirit calmly responded, "Very well, but know that it is as if you are invited to a superb banquet and you refuse to eat."

How right he was…his sentence, filled with common sense and stripped of judgment, caught my attention and stayed in my mind for a long time. He was the first priest who seemed honest and did not impose requirements on me. We had already had an interview with one of the priests of the Colmar cathedral, who had insisted on having us sign a paper obliging us to educate our future children in the Catholic faith. Horrified, we fled and left him flushed with fury, with his pen and oath sheet in hand. Once again, I had not understood the purposes behind such demands and once again I was outraged. How can one believe that we can impose a relationship with God? How dare you ask to sign a promise, which if not kept, would make us guilty of lying? I thought that if God existed, He was Love and Freedom...It was then unthinkable that Jacques and I would fall into the trap of these priests.

We got married on June 20, 1975, in the cathedral, me in a white dress. But, as we had already informed the priest, we refused the blessing and communion. We were honest rebels.

Chapter Four

The Cherub

On December 30, 1978, I gave birth to a beautiful baby boy, Frantz, a healthy baby with honey-colored eyes.

A week earlier, this little life in me stirred strongly and began to move towards the exit. When we rushed to the hospital, everything was organized to welcome the baby. But Frantz, already a joker, decided to stay warm and calm in his protective shelter. So bassinet, sleeping bags and toiletries in hand, we returned home, disappointed not to already hold in our arms the fruit of our love. Finally, two weeks later, our baby, curious about the world and perhaps also eager to see his parents' faces, appeared and put an end to our impatience.

Jacques was present throughout the delivery and he picked up the baby in his large, reassuring open hands. I looked at father and son and couldn't help but think that this six-foot-tall man had also started out as a little piece of humanity. Later our son would have the majestic stature of his father. Upon his arrival, Frantz gestured and cried out signifying his good health and his desire for life. Eyes misty with tears, his voice choked with emotion, Jacques gently placed our son on my chest and whispered: "Look, how beautiful he is; he is the most beautiful of all the babies in the world! But how small he is!"

Having had my baby at the age of thirty undoubtedly concerned me. Intimidated, I dared not touch him for fear of hurting him. So, back home, Jacques took matters into his own hands and took care of him, changing him, washing him, and giving him the bottles I prepared. I loved watching them together and wondered how such a strong man could care for such a fragile little being without breaking it. I was a mother full of love and tenderness, but not a practical mom, and I was nervous.

Before setting off again, Jacques taught me the basics of childcare and reassured me, and I saw that I was quite capable of it all. I then experienced the immense joy of taking care of my baby, touching him, and covering him with hugs and kisses--we were quite a pair!

The arrival of our son created in me a sense of unity, a new balance, like an accomplishment. The circle was perfectly closed. My life as a woman was becoming a harmonious symphony, culminating with this fragile little being making me a mother, with his father at my side. As a result, I forever left my desire to wander and my search for love. I anchored myself in a full and balanced life with the two men in my life. The future appeared to be full of promise and happiness.

When Frantz was fifteen months old, Jacques needed to learn English for his new job with an American oil company, so we moved to England where we rented a small cottage in Hindead, Surrey, and lived there for almost three years. Frantz's first words were spoken in Shakespeare's language, with an irresistible French accent, before he was two years old.

Our lives were punctuated by the departures of Jacques to the countries of black gold: Africa, Indonesia, Iran, and Iraq. After six weeks of exhausting work, he came back to us exhausted but overjoyed to be reunited with us. Then we would resume our little life together. I would make High Teas with cookies and sandwiches, and we would go picnicking in the English countryside. There, we would meet deer, wild rabbits, and squirrels by the hundreds. Our circle of English friends was expanding every month. The kindness of their welcome was rewarded by French dinners we prepared: blanquette of veal, a beef stew. Wines scrupulously chosen by Jacques undoubtedly had something to do with their fondness for us! Or maybe they just liked us for ourselves.

Our house was full of laughter and children with muddy boots up to their knees, mischievous and happy. But Jacques's regular departures were more and more difficult for Frantz and me.

One day, on the way back from taking Jacques to Heathrow airport, as I was lost in my melancholy thoughts, I felt little arms circling my neck: "Mommy, don't worry, I am going to take care of you now… Mom, don't worry, I'll take care of you now…"

My little "bulldozer" with a tender heart was comfortable in his position as head of the house during Jacques' absences. With his sensitivity and his delicate instinct, he understood my dismay and sadness and reassured me of his caring and compassionate presence. My sweet little fellow, sometimes quite mischievous too, knew how to give me the courage and the patience to endure until his father's return. He assured me of his protective support with determination, starting at the tender age of three.

These years in England were full of life, friendships, children, birds, cats, and growing together as a family. Our cloudless sky heralded a smooth future. Frantz grew and became most handsome, with his almond-shaped eyes and his playful face. Although shy, he amassed many girlfriends, who fell in love with his French allure and inimitable French accent when he spoke English, as well as his British accent when he spoke French. He was one of those children no one could resist liking. As with all mothers, he was, for me, the most beautiful and attractive of all the little boys in the world. He greatly resembled his father in his athletic physique and daring character.

The three of us loved each other with undying love and we relished the times we were together. Our flourishing health and bank account reflected the strength of a carefree life.

When a friend asked me which church we went to, I replied lightly that, for me, God did not exist, but that if he did exist, good for him! So we were confident that life was going well, and we could assuredly face whatever may come.

What foolish contempt, what ridiculous smugness, what unspeakable stupidity, and what arrogance! I didn't want God, but that didn't mean he didn't want me. I had given up on him for over twenty years, but that didn't prove that he had given up on me! I understood much later that the God of the Bible, incarnated in Jesus, "Emmanuel," "God with us," was with me, even if I totally ignored him; even if I did not want to be with him. I had opened the door of my heart to Jesus at the age of eight, and it was an eternal commitment to him. Jesus had paid the ultimate price, so that one day I would return to the bosom of the Father. *"If we are faithless, he will remain faithful, for he cannot disown himself."* (2 Timothy 2:13)

"Shema Israel...Shema Ariane..." God called me, as he has called his people, Israel, throughout the Bible. "Listen Israel...listen Ariane..." But I heard nothing. Deaf, selfish, and superficial, I did not recognize the little flame in me, smothered by so many weeds, on which the creator had breathed.

The months passed slowly, marked by the returns of Jacques, whom we greeted with all the joy and emotion that the long weeks of waiting had provoked. Our little boy was growing up with no particular problems, except for some difficulty falling asleep and the restless nights of nightmares that left him distressed for several hours. The English doctor explained to me that this was probably because it was not easy for such a small child to learn two languages at the same time. Indeed, Frantz went to an English school while we spoke French at home. So, we decided to communicate, as much as possible, in English between the three of us. It was a challenge that we gladly accepted for the love of our little guy, and the desire to have more peaceful nights! Without knowing it, we were living a blessed life filled with grace.

It was during this time that Frantz said to me in a bold voice, "Mom, I will never be grown up. Besides, I don't want to grow up." Seven years later, we would look back at his pronouncement as dramatically prophetic.

These words resonated in my heart, like the foreshadowing of an implacable danger I knew nothing about, but which would come back to me later as the echo of the warning of terrible news. A red light had come on, which I immediately swept away. Children say so many things...

"Why do you say that?" I asked, puzzled.

He didn't reply. There was nothing to say. His hazel-colored eyes looked a little sad. Children's intuitions are very strange and sometimes turn out to be true.

I took him on my lap and kissed him. Then, with the agility of a squirrel on his branch, he jumped down to rejoin his Legos, his toy cars, and his safe universe. Our carefree life resumed, and all was right with the world. Frantz was in great health, so why panic over a few childish words?

Part Two: The Unbearable

Chapter Five

Migratory Birds

Although we were very satisfied living in the country of Shakespeare, one day our craziness, our need for sun, and a yearning to move began to tickle us. Entrusting Frantz to my sister, Marie-Laure, we both went to America to determine the possibility of establishing ourselves there. Everything was big: their ice cream cones, their freeways, their welcomes, and their smiles. This first impression of overflowing conviviality, openness to others, energy, and efficiency suited us perfectly. We concluded—a bit hastily no doubt—that it was the ideal country for our appetite for adventure. We determined to do everything possible to return to America with Frantz a few months later and to settle there. But after navigating many obstacles to obtaining our visas, our project, however well put together, fell through. Depressed at the idea of having to give up living in such a welcoming country, we changed our plans and headed for Alsace in France.

As the months passed, we became more embedded in this Alsatian land where life is so good. We quickly bought an apartment in Colmar, which gave us the feeling of being settled, even though we were more like migratory birds.

At that time, we often went for walks in the Vosges, where Frantz liked to climb rocks and hills, run on the paths hidden behind trees, and watch for wild animals. Our little boy loved life, which he wanted full and intense; he enjoyed everything a child of his age could hope for. His adoring parents loved him unconditionally.

But in 1981, an oil crash suddenly clouded the assurance of a cloudless sky. The price of a barrel of oil collapsed drastically, leading to an end of the oil exploration and extraction boom. The drilling companies laid off workers in waves and a few months later, Jacques returned home for good. There was no question for him of unemployment insurance, social security, or various safety nets, since, by choosing to work for an American company, he and our family had given up French social protections.

We had always been more spendthrift than frugal. Now, the time had come to pay the price.

How could Frantz be protected as much as possible from this storm, which we knew would at least destabilize us for a while, if not overwhelm us? We had to try to stay strong and put our energy and intelligence into finding a solution.

This difficult period of life lasted one year. I shook every time Frantz sneezed, knowing that none of us were covered by health insurance. Jacques came back from the mailbox each day, his eyes increasingly sad. The oil crisis would be long, and job opportunities in oil exploration and drilling were scarce. With no blue on the horizon, the sky had turned dark and ominous.

We kept expenses as low as possible: heating and food expenditures were reduced to basic necessities, except when my mother visited us with a big roast! We ran out of savings after a few months. Next, we were the victims of a scam which led to a trial. Life seemed determined to give us no gifts!

But one morning, when we no longer held out much hope for the future, Jacques returned from the mailbox with a letter in his hand and declared brightly, his eyes shining with hope: "Ariane, I think this is the end of our slump."

I had tears in my eyes as I read the job offers from two French drilling companies.

One was a job as a site manager in Africa for water drilling, while the other would allow Jacques to return to his profession as a black gold driller. A few days later, having chosen oil, he left for Indonesia.

We were again full of optimism and energy, happy to be alive, even if we had to get used to Jacques' extended absences again. As before, our little guy let out a sad sigh when he saw his dad disappear behind the airport boarding gate, then snuggled up to me and whispered sadly: "Are we starting to count the days again, Mom?"

He had grown up, but still needed the affection and assurance that his father gave him.

During this year of unemployment, life had proven to us that it was certainly not "a long quiet river." Yet through these unsettling lessons, we understood that we had to find another solution if we wanted to keep Jacques in France. His departures increasingly weighed on us. His twelve years in the oil business had meant seventy-two months of absence! In other words, half of his life had been away from us. We both found that this was too much!

He wanted to see his son grow up, and Frantz needed to feel the secure presence of his father, to play with him, and also to measure his strength in tough battles where, bodies intertwined, they both rolled laughing on the carpet in the living room. For my part, I also wanted my husband at home and wanted to become a full-time wife, which, to this point, I had never been able to be, since Jacques had become a driller a few months before our marriage.

During one of his stays in Africa, when we were separated by thousands of kilometers, we remembered the success of a French bakery in England, and we both had the same sweet idea: *Why not learn how to bake bread?* I thought. *Why not learn how to bake croissants?* Jacques said to himself on his platform. This new plan for a bakery would be the perfect alternative to the absences of the oil business and would ensure that the three of us lived together. Then once the bakery inevitably succeeded, we believed with the unconscious audacity of beginners, we would sell it and move to Australia. Our impulse to move took over. We had missed out on America, but we would succeed in Australia!

No sooner said than done, our goal was set! But since we were not in the bakery business yet, two things were essential: we had to obtain a certificate from the Chamber of Commerce and raise the start-up capital. We decided that Jacques would continue his work on the oil rig and that I would do an internship organized by the City of Colmar and as train in a bakery.

A Turkish shoemaker's stall soon caught our attention which, because of its location right across from the Colmar technical high school, guaranteed success. 3,000 hungry students were an important clientele base to help us reach our goal with flying colors! We put all our eggs in this basket, renovating the premises and enthusiastically opening the Croissanterie in November 1987.

The first day was a disaster. We had carefully arranged magnificent croissants, golden brown, crispy, plump pain au chocolat, as well as other pastries, baked to perfection, prominently in the display case. But no one came in the entire day. Disappointed, we pretended to wash the coffee cups from which no one had sipped and the plates that no one had used. We even wiped down tables at which no customers had lingered.

Out of the corner of our eyes, as discreetly as possible, we watched the students passing in front of the Croissanterie, with grown-ups: "Oh, how beautiful! Cool!" But neither the warm, inviting setting, nor the delicious smell of warm croissants made anyone sit down for even a moment. Earnings on this first day were catastrophic. It seemed like we were headed for a small business fiasco.

We had planned everything, except that we had not accounted for human beings' strong force of habit. Students usually left high school during recess and ran directly to the small bakery right next to ours. People don't change their routines very quickly!

That evening, as we were taking stock of that disastrous day, for the first time I saw my husband demoralized, his eyes downcast and cloudy. I suspected that he felt responsible for this venture, which now seemed insane to him, and felt guilty for having dragged his little family to the edge of ruin. I was not feeling successful either, but I wanted to encourage him anyway. I also needed to hold on to the hope for better days. My desire to help gave me the right words, and the more I spoke, the more

I convinced myself—we had to be patient and stay calm. We had come too far to just give up. We had to continue towards the goal we had set for ourselves, to make this Croissanterie a success, sell it, and with the money from the sale, go and settle in Perth, Australia. It's well-known that Australians love French croissants! We were very familiar with the story of "Perrette and her Pail of Milk," by Jean de la Fontaine.

After a few days, we realized that every morning a few customers were waiting for the 8:00 a.m. opening. As we didn't want to disappoint an emerging clientele, we decided to open earlier and earlier until we settled on the earliest legal time of 4:00 a.m.!

We quickly became the meeting point for late-night party people from Colmar and the surrounding area, thanks to our hot croissants ready before dawn. We welcomed club outings and their staff. An hour later, the teams of night shift workers arrived who were finishing their night's work, followed by those who, in contrast, were just starting their work days. Then the paramedics and city staff would stop for a *little black* or a café au lait. Around six in the morning, I would often box up a dozen croissants, which a nurse in a hurry would carefully take to treat her colleagues.

Later, as the sun rose, a host of people would wander in, becoming regulars over time, and some even becoming friends. I liked this melting pot of people with such different origins, educations, and experiences.

Sometimes there were people newly released from jail, petty thieves; sometimes nightclub bouncers would come in, as well as rowdy night clubbers who had been kicked out because of violence or drunkenness. In this late-night underworld, we learned a certain language as well as the behavior essential to manage what nightclub doormen call "drunk meat!"

Our early morning work hours forced us to hire an au pair to take care of Frantz. Indeed, we had to be fully committed to the business, sacrificing our family life a little, sparing neither our time nor our efforts. That was the price to pay, we would sleep later!

During the weekend, an impressive line of cars awaited the opening. And Sunday morning showed excellent sales, with the register exploding!

The Croissanterie had become an astounding success, well beyond what we had imagined. Until 7:00 a.m., the little eighty-square-meter space was packed. Friendships were made there and news was shared; it was the place to be.

The projected, but seemingly impossible, amount of income that Jacques had announced to our dubious accountant, was not only reached but often exceeded.

So I dreamed of the Australia that awaited us, that different and exhilarating new life. I thought of our little guy, Frantz, our beautiful boy, who would become Franco-Australian. I thought of how easily he would adapt since English would come back to him quickly. I dreamed of my mother, who loved traveling so much, coming to see us. We would invite family and friends to stay at our big house by the sea. I pictured our new life together, without separations, without the calendar with dates marked in red to indicate Jacques' departures. My desire to travel with my husband and my son was going to come true. We were so tired of those cycles of melancholy due to separations, and then of excessive gaiety—of this schizophrenia of the heart.

The future was smiling upon us. "I could see myself already…" sang Aznavour. Me too! I imagined the country of kangaroos, with vast open spaces with horizons so far away that the earth and the sky merged. A land with wild animals and people whom we would not fail to charm with our croissants and French accents.

Life, smiling and cheerful, awaited us.

Chapter Six

Lightning Strikes

February 10, 1988. That day, everything collapsed.

We arrived at the Croissanterie at the usual time as the smell of fresh coffee and hot croissants quickly enticed the first customers. Later in the morning Petra, our Austrian au pair, took Frantz to school. Nothing extraordinary that day, only the familiar ritual of early mornings in Colmar.

The day before our son had seemed tired and a little pale, having spent a week's vacation in the Austrian mountains where Petra, who had become like a big sister to him, had invited him.

When I asked him about his athletic prowess, I found out he had only gone skiing one day during the whole week, and feeling sad and nauseous, he had not left Petra's parents' family hotel. This unusual behavior was blamed on a stomachache resulting from eating too many chocolates. Yet when Frantz refused to join his Boy Scout buddies and chose to spend the last day of his vacation on his bed leafing through comics, I sensed something was wrong and thought about seeing our family doctor.

This first day of our calamity is a bit foggy in my mind. Frantz went to school, but I was told he had refused to eat lunch and that he had remained seated on the playground. The orange warning lights in my brain from the day before turned to bright red, setting off my already alert maternal instinct even more. Distraught, I went to the school immediately and found him outside the classroom, where, exhausted, he showed me his neck which was ringed by a series of subcutaneous nodules like a collar.

Panicked, I took him straight to our family doctor who examined him and with a very worried look and requested an immediate blood test.

From that day forward, I sank into a spiral of anguish where each event pierced my heart a little deeper.

My first thoughts were that he had mononucleosis, but our doctor whispered in a grave voice, "It's much more serious: Frantz has leukemia. Currently, children with this disease have a 30% chance of survival. He must go to the Strasbourg hospital tomorrow. I have done what is necessary. He will be admitted to the Hautepierre CHU in the oncology department. Show up as soon as possible with this cover letter; they are waiting for you."

In a state of shock, I suddenly felt nauseated. I quickly fled, stunned by the inhuman brutality of this tragic news. Crossing the street like a mad person, I heard the car horns, then leaned over the bridge and watched the river flow peacefully as a tornado of distress erupted inside me. I wanted to dive into it, thinking I would not have the courage to endure the days to come.

I finally gathered the little strength that remained in me and went to give Jacques the news. I parked the car right in front of our Croissanterie, but I couldn't go any further. The news was unbearable and I was so paralyzed that I could not repeat what I had just been told. After a few moments, through the fog of my tears, I saw Jacques cross the street.

"What's wrong with him, what's wrong with him? Say something!"

Burning to know and already worried by the doctor's desire not to tell us anything over the phone, his gaze shone with worry and uncertainty over what he sensed at the sight of my red eyes and silence: something dreadful had descended over our lives. I looked at him intently without daring to tell him the terrible news, as if to hang on to our life before, if only for a few more seconds.

I rejected the diagnosis with all my being and did not want to formalize the disease by speaking of it out loud, as if not verbalizing it would mean that our little boy was still healthy. I had the unbearable feeling that I could no longer protect Frantz as I had done all these years. But despite everything, I could not escape the truth and I stammered: "Frantz has the worst disease, it's the worst Jacques, it's the worst…He has leukemia."

I burst into tears.

In my world where everything was going well, in our world of healthy people, I was not aware that there are many terrible illnesses, even worse ones. That day, we entered the school of suffering—that of anguish, despair, and extreme sadness. We would have six months to do our classes, six months of trauma with very little positive news.

Chapter Seven

The Cyclone

We arrived at the hospital holding our little boy. I still tried to believe it was all a mistake as I had done the day before, rushing to the laboratory, clinging to the idea of a possible mix-up in the processing of the files, despite the irrefutable evidence of the disease.

But faced with the sad expressions of the laboratory assistants confirming the diagnosis, I rushed to Frantz's former pediatrician to get a second opinion, still not wanting to believe it. He was a good, gracious man who I thought could advise me or better yet, wake me from this horrible nightmare. But he was on vacation, and I found myself alone in tears on the sidewalk. In my panic, I bought kiwi fruit, foolishly thinking of saving my son with vitamin-packed fruit to fight the cancer. I don't remember anything else about that day except my distress and total inability to cope with it.

Yet it was necessary!

Frantz had received the news of his hospitalization with concern, but also with relative calm. We assured him that we would always be with him, and when he was cured everything would go on as before. I explained to him gently that we had to go to Strasbourg so he could get the best treatment possible. He trusted us completely, but I knew I was powerless to save him from the suffering to come.

He was just ten years old when he slipped into a world of frightening heaviness, where his blood cell scores were more important than his school grades had ever been. Jacques and I were thrown abruptly into a bitter fight to win a battle in which the weapons did not belong to us.

As soon as we arrived at the hospital ward, we were greeted by the oncologist who would take care of our son. The spinal tap was excruciating
for Frantz. He cried out in pain as we held him by the shoulders, as we
had been instructed. As we tried to encourage him as best as we could, I
saw drops of sweat beading on Jacques' forehead. The doctor was getting
angry, the stressed nurses were watching me closely and my mother, who
had insisted on coming along to support us, wiped away the tears she could
not hold back. This first contact with the oncology service immediately
chilled me. Watching others suffer, I guess, the less sensitive get used to it,
and wanting to protect themselves, some caregivers lose all empathy. This
service had no soul and, very quickly, I knew we would not be entitled to
any compassion.

Frantz was put in a room where we waited all day for the results of
the spinal tap and the latest blood tests. At the end of the afternoon, the
doctor's conclusions snatched away the few crumbs of hope we had clung
to: "There is no doubt, your little boy has acute lymphoblastic leukemia.
The chemotherapy protocol must be put in place as a matter of urgency;
the procedure for the catheter is scheduled for tomorrow morning. Sign
the waiver for us to get started."

After hearing some information about our son's illness and how the
doctor was planning to treat him, I realized that that was all she could
give us. I had the bitter impression that I hadn't found an ally with whom
we could fight Frantz's leukemia, but just a technician doing her job. The
tone was set: they would take care of our child because it was their job, but
we shouldn't expect any more. My judgment unfortunately turned out to
be correct.

Later we learned that in some health institutions, death is fought with
the same weapons, but instead of being dismissed as defeat, it is accepted
as the last stage of life. Unfortunately, we did not have the chance to go
through this ordeal in those conditions.

The Croissanterie continued to operate. I was leaving at dawn for
the hospital and Jacques would join me during the day. At first, Frantz
responded well to the chemotherapy treatment, and I was amazed to see

him come to terms with his lot with such grace. Sometimes I would take him out in the halls for a walk. He would then push his IV pole under the gaze of sick adults who smiled sadly at him and mumbled a few words wearily. It was so depressing that we quickly went back to his room, to pick up the Lego constructions and the Scrabble games. The three of us built a little world of our own. His father and I tried to laugh and play as naturally as possible. In the hospital lobby, Jacques had unearthed a book of jokes he was reading to his son and their mingled laughter was helping me endure.

For my part, I feverishly read articles dealing with alternative natural medicine, such as "Dealing with Cancer" and "Healing with Plants." I thought that once he was cured I would have to learn how to cook all over again, using different ingredients, and stop eating or drinking various things. This experience of serious and fatal illness would give us another impetus: a healthier way of life. As my son played or fell asleep in his father's arms, peaceful and secure, I thought of how I loved them both with undying love, and nothing could separate us.

Despite the medical team's lack of communication and compassion, I had confidence in the treatments they offered. I did not let myself think about the odds of success, only wanting to imagine a complete and triumphant recovery.

When the diagnosis was made, we were suddenly plunged into a frightening daze. Then, once we got over the shock and regained our necessary composure, we began the fight. Trying to reassure ourselves, we told each other that our little boy had always been in good health and that with the treatment protocol in place and his parents by his side, he had to win this battle. Love would inevitably triumph over disease.

The results of the first rounds of chemotherapy gave us hope that we were on the right path: that of rediscovered happiness where our unit of three would finally be reconstituted: Jacques, Frantz, and Ariane were a whole, and nobody and nothing could tear our child away from us. We had the strength and the conviction to believe we could defeat it. It was the natural role of parents—Jacques and I would fully invest in this battle for our son.

At the onset of Frantz's disease, we were so certain of his cure that we didn't pass up on the opportunity to expand our business by buying the nearby bakery. Planning for the future also felt like warding off the curse and increasing Frantz's chances of recovery.

Jacques and I shared the anguish of our child's illness intimately, maintaining a smile and optimism, despite the attacks of panic that regularly hit us. Frantz would be cured and we would go far away, leaving behind infusions, needle jabs, chemo, and all of the pain. I surprised myself, imagining a son and a father balancing on surfboards on the crest of the Australian waves, not doubting that Jacques, who had been the European surfing champion for twelve years, would introduce his son to the sport of his childhood.

A few weeks passed. Frantz was still that whimsical and lively little boy whose hair had not fallen out after the first rounds of chemo. We had brought his toys, stuffed animals, and drawings to his hospital room to recreate the atmosphere of home. Sometimes, exhausted after a night's work, Jacques would fall asleep, book in hand, while I dozed off on the bathroom tiles.

I forced myself to put on a calm face and a convincing smile, to tell Frantz that the next spinal tap would not be as painful as the previous one had been, and that the disease would be conquered. I had to be strong for our little boy who was fighting so bravely, and also for his father who was determined to stay strong for his son and for me. We were in a cruel battle, the outcome of which also depended upon in the fierceness of our love.

But love is not always enough.

In the evening as I left the hospital, the tears I could not hold back, flowed with abandon. I no longer had to put on my game face or pretend, so all the way back to Colmar, I screamed in pain.

After eight weeks of treatment, the results were good enough for the medical team to consider letting us return home for the Easter holidays.

The doctor told us that our son was in remission. He could therefore go home as long as his temperature was monitored, and he would return to the hospital immediately at the slightest sign of a fever. That day, we were also pleasantly surprised to hear that if everything continued on well, our son would no longer be hospitalized but would become an outpatient for a year, and then we could possibly talk about being cured.

We left the hospital with light hearts, following Frantz who walked quickly, holding his teddy bear. He would turn around every now and then, as if to make sure he was wide awake. I had the impression that we were becoming "real" again, that we had emerged from the nightmare. The April sun, the people around us, and the departure from Strasbourg, with our son this time, symbolized the promise of returning to life. I felt like we had come a long way, that we had come to the edge of excruciating peril, but that the storm was receding. I was confident in the future and in my son's recovery. My protective love and treatment had been stronger than the disease.

Gifts awaited Frantz at the house. We would celebrate Easter with my mother, who was delighted with her grandson's homecoming. Champagne in the fridge and a good lunch helped us to celebrate the beginning of our victory. These few days of joy after all the ordeals eased our permanent state of tension a little and let us look to the future with more hope.

Chapter Eight

The Earthquake

I anxiously checked Frantz's temperature every evening since, despite the relief of being at home, I did not forget "the sword of Damocles" hovering over us. So, when, on the day before his return appointment with the oncologist, the thermometer read over 102 degrees, I thought I would faint. My throat, dry with emotion and my heart drowning in sobs, I tried to calm down by telling myself that he had played a lot in the garden and had simply gotten overheated. I could not accept a recurrence of the blood cancer, and I categorically refused the reappearance of this monster in our lives. Frantz stretched out on his bed and leafed through a magazine as if to escape my panic-stricken gaze. I took his temperature every half-hour but the thermometer, without fail, indicated the same, fateful temperature of 102 degrees. Panicking, I was stunned by worry about the gravity of the situation, which my little boy had perhaps also grasped. My mother and Jacques were devastated when I told them the news, which was as startling as it was unexpected.

The next day, in the waiting room of the hospital, I still tried to believe it was just a broken thermometer. Against all logic, I was trying to convince myself that in some cases a fever may not be an indicator of the return of the disease and that the finger prick in the morning, allowing for a drop of blood, was going to prove it. I couldn't admit the reality of the tragedy that was brewing and everything in me reared up to postpone the inevitable. Yet, when the doctor asked to speak to Jacques alone, I suddenly had the ominous feeling of great misfortune and the terrible sense of having failed my mission as a protective mother. With my defensive heart,

I realized we were going to fail, and I knew I was incapable of going through this dark valley.

Frantz and I were finally allowed to join Jacques in the doctor's office, whose body language I tried to read during the consultation. But she remained placid and professional in her white blouse, preventing me from picking up any clues.

Going down to the hospital pharmacy, Jacques signaled to me not to question him in front of Frantz. He was given medication which I would later know were pills to "help his wife to sleep." My son was on his way to death, and all the doctors had to offer me were sleeping pills! When Frantz was going to undergo all kinds of physical and mental suffering, would my role be limited to sleeping properly? Were the sedatives meant to calm me down? To avoid suffering? Even today, I am shocked at this failure to help people in such dire need. On the contrary, I hoped that my anguish would be taken into account with an attitude of compassion and not judgment. I wanted to be told about exceptions and miracles, that there was no need for me to medicate myself with drugs to escape the drama into which my son had been plunged.

Jacques never gave me the pills. He knew my distaste for this form of escape, which some people may need, but which, in our case, signaled cowardice. We would stay with our little fellow until the end, and still seek to save him.

Frantz sadly resumed his way to his hospital room, but this time the treatment was redoubled; we were moving up a stage, with a new, more aggressive protocol and devastating side effects. The conversation that Jacques had had with the doctor was unequivocal: the serious relapse left hardly any hope. Yet the medical team wanted to try something again, and we agreed not to give up the fight. Frantz's body reacted violently to the aggressive chemotherapy that caused vomiting until his throat and insides were raw. These sessions left him pale and bloodless.

Due to his aplastic anaemia, he was transferred to a sterile room to avoid any bacterial contamination. Now we had to put on personal protective equipment to approach our son: pants, blouse, slippers, hat, and mask.

The green color of these garments did not inspire hope. In this strange pageantry, only our voices, our eyes, and our hands could lavish caresses and encouragement and transmit our tenderness and love to him. No one dared to come to see us. No one entered this room, except a hospital staff member in the same costume, who automatically replaced bottles of chemo or other products when Frantz pressed a button communicating with the nurses' station. The days passed, darker and darker, and the weeks were only interrupted by blood tests and punctures, the results of which showed no sign of improvement.

On July 14, the French National holiday, when the sky began to darken and I had long passed my allotted time, I advised Frantz to watch the fireworks through the windows after I left. He had enjoyed the ones from the previous year in Colmar very much, so I naively thought that it may break his loneliness for a moment. Raising his sad eyes to me, he answered softly, "Mom I'm not interested in any of that anymore; I just want to get out of here; I want to go home."

The last days had been particularly painful for him, so I dared to ask his doctor to let me spend the night in the armchair next to his bed. But the refusal of this frozen-hearted woman was non-negotiable: "This isn't his last night; I can't make an exception. Come back tomorrow," she blurted out briefly. Then she grabbed a file and walked out of her office, turning her back to me.

I left the hospital shaking with rage and pain. In the car, in revolt, I screamed my sadness and my despair, I screamed my helplessness, I screamed out my inability to accept my son's suffering. As I could no longer see the road through my tears, I parked somehow on the sidewalk and began to vomit and sob, unable to stop.

At the end of July, as soon as I arrived at the hospital, the nurses asked me to go upstairs immediately for a consultation with Frantz's doctor. As soon as I sat down, her unfriendly voice intoned, "We can try a bone marrow transplant, but after that is over, I won't do anything else. The latest analysis is catastrophic. If you or your husband are compatible, we'll talk about that. Take a blood test on an empty stomach." So, we did the next morning. But this hope was also refused to us because our blood groups proved to be incompatible. We then listened to the doctor's last words, which finally opened our hearts: "There is nothing more to do, you can take your son away; I prescribed him antidepressants and pain medication. Come back to refill them." That was basically all we were told that day. Terrified by the news of my child's imminent death, I jumped up and paced back and forth in a panic in the doctor's office. Unperturbed, but annoyed, she ordered me to sit down and calm down. Her indifference and her coldness nailed me to the chair.

We returned to Colmar and the big house that Frantz loved so much, but its atmosphere had changed now that he had lost his innocence and knew what real pain was. His sad, serious gaze unmistakably revealed his experiences with suffering and seemed to shout to me: "Help me, do something!"

The feeling of helplessness was choking me. I slept badly and little; I tried desperately to act without knowing what to do. The Strasbourg hospital sent us off with a few pills, so we absolutely had to find another place to treat Frantz. We couldn't watch our little boy die without doing anything further. I did not accept his death sentence. I would not allow him to go to an unknown elsewhere. I refused to let him leave us. I was already thinking of sending him to another hospital.

Chapter Nine

The Black Hole

S ome days later, I found out about an emeritus professor of cancer in Paris. This man of science might have found a new treatment of which Strasbourg doctors were unaware. I wanted to continue the fight, not to give up. I wanted to go to the best doctors.

After stubborn pressure and several telephone conversations, the three of us drove to his office in August. We had explained to Frantz that the new doctor in Paris specialized in his disease and knew of better treatments for him. Jacques would stay with us for a day or two, then he would go back to work at the Croissanterie. The brand-new department of Professors Mathé and Schwartzenberg had just opened, and I better understood the enormous difficulties we had had in getting our son admitted. The demand was such that the patients were handpicked. The large bay windows of the sterile rooms overlooked the hallway where families could see their sick loved ones. The only communication possible was through the telephone located on either side of the glass partition. This was an all-out war on any microbial intrusion and the patients, cut off from the outside world, looked like very rare exotic fish in a fish tank…Frantz became the smallest of them.

We looked at our little boy through the window, speaking to him only by gesture or over the phone. It was unbearable. We forced ourselves to hold back our tears and smile at him anyway. Jacques did his best to find a few jokes to tell, but the words and intonations had a hard time getting through the telephone line, at the end of which Frantz listened with an increasingly distracted ear.

As for me, utterly helpless, I could not find any words to comfort him.

As we had decided, Jacques returned to Colmar. I was staying in Paris at my mother's apartment, which I left at dawn to find Frantz behind his window. This situation was unbearable, yet I still clung to the idea that I would find hope for a cure in Villejuif Hospital. Little by little, my son slipped into a sort of lethargy and detachment. He wanted it to stop, as I desperately continued to believe in these cutting-edge treatments—and life—to the end.

One morning, the psychologist of the service summoned me and told me abruptly that my son was "temperamental." Frantz had refused an ice-cold water bottle during the night and sent it flying on the ground. I also learned that his fever had reached over104 degrees could not be controlled, and that the night staff, at their wit's end, had opted for the cold-water solution. I continue to be amazed by this young psychologist allowing herself to talk about "temperament" on the part of a child in his sixth month of battling leukemia! Anyone would have understood that this was certainly not the time for me to listen to that kind of judgment, already offensive to any mother, and so needlessly hurtful and cruel to a mom whose little boy was going to die soon.

This extremely high temperature made us fall that day into an irreversible danger zone which triggered in me the beginnings of "letting go." In this high-tech department, at the forefront of research and progress, my little ten-year-old boy might not be cured. He was getting worse each day, and had the absent, sad air of a lamb resigned to his fate. On the fourth day of hospitalization, I was granted special permission: I was able to enter my son's room for a huge hug, and even obtained permission to bathe him. Happy with this moment stolen from the "fishbowl," he bravely smiled. In the small room where the bathtub was installed by compassionate nurses, I felt so happy about this special moment for us. My eyes and my hands were the only parts of me in the open air. Through my mask, I spoke to him softly. Using a large sponge, I slid the water down his neck and over his shoulders. I massaged his back and his legs. I took his hands gently and kissed him hard; I was almost as wet as he was. It was a very sweet moment, a parenthesis of tenderness and complicity, a snub to the illness. We both felt a bit like we were at home, with the water that calms and purifies. I closed my eyes, and as I dried him, I thought of the slowly draining bathwater, unfortunately not dragging the malignant cells away with it. We came back to the room where a gentle nurse overlooked the fact of my overstay with "the patient."

Later, as I passed through the treatment room, I saw a board with the names of the patients and their medical programs. My son's name was written there with a change in treatment for the next day. I immediately asked to speak with the head of the team, who met me in the room where families and caregivers left their sterile clothes every evening. "The doctor prescribed your child a new protocol of chemotherapy with another chemical cocktail added," she said uneasily.

I wanted to continue the fight, of course, but also to have confidence in it. I had to talk to the doctor before anything started. Very early the next day, I crossed the corridor into the sterile section where the eminent professor's colleague awaited me like a benevolent white phantom. Her feminine, warm, and pleasant voice did me good, and when I asked for detailed information on the development of the situation, that voice with beautiful brown eyes softened even more, and then her eyes darkened.

"I am sincerely very sorry to tell you, madam, that the last results leave me with no hope. We have studied Frantz's case at length with the professor. But since you came from Strasbourg and you insisted that a new treatment be considered, we will try a new chemotherapy anyway, if you give us your consent."

"What are his chances? And what will be the side effects of this new treatment?" I stammered in a whisper.

Her eyes filled with tears, and I heard the death verdict:

"There is no more chance. This new chemo is extremely harsh, and we have no control over the side effects."

My legs weren't carrying me anymore... "Here we are," I thought in a flash. "We are at the end." My tears quickly flooded the mask behind which I breathed, "What would you do in my place, Doctor, if Frantz were your son?"

Her gaze, which showed all the compassion in the world, fixed on me intensely while two tears traced a furrow on the mask hiding her face. Overwhelmed by her response as much as moved by her empathy, I heard, with a shattered heart, the fatal observation. "If Frantz were my little boy, I would stop everything. If I were in your place, I would not cause him further suffering, unnecessarily...I am sorry." she added, her trembling voice overcome with sadness. Then, slowly turning away, she disappeared down the hall. I immediately decided to put everything on hold to think it over. I had to phone Jacques...and find help for Frantz somewhere else.

I had missed the mark; the cure was not here either. I was not responsible for the failure, but knowing the ugly truth, I would be guilty of adding unnecessary days of suffering to it.

This doctor with a tender and compassionate gaze had weakened my courage. I had no more strength, no more energy or desire to fight. My son was at the end of his life; I was at the end of hope.

Then, after calming myself down and wiping my eyes, I joined Frantz in his room where I told him he would be leaving the fishbowl soon and we would finally go home. He didn't answer and didn't even ask if he was cured or if more treatment was needed. His wry silence and his sad little smile were probably the first signs of his understanding of the situation.

As I left him that evening, my heart was torn by the choice I had just made. Taking our little boy away from the barbaric instruments and therapies that made him suffer for nothing also represented an acceptance of his death, against which his father and I had fought with all our might for five and a half months.

It was a surrender. I knew this decision was dictated by love, but I couldn't bear to think that it led to death, the last stage of his short life. The fatal verdict that I would not accept in Strasbourg, came back to my heart, vengeful and ruthless. There was no escaping it any longer.

Jacques still wanted to discuss it and jumped on the first train. Around midnight we were hugging each other, sobbing breathlessly. I heard the beating of his panicked heart and he listened to mine as we shared in the same unspeakable suffering.

At dawn, the conviction that we were doing the best for our son led us to make the most difficult decision we had ever had to make: we would stop all medical treatments and only administer painkillers.

The next morning we both went to the hospital where Frantz was as surprised as he was happy to see his father. We informed the nurses of our decision to organize his discharge from the hospital as quickly as possible. Everything was done to ensure that he was in the best possible shape for travel. After a long transfusion of blood and a whole series of medications, he did indeed seem to regain some strength with his cheeks flushed.

I was happy, but also desperate to take him because, with the failure of this last "rescue" plan at Villejuif Hospital, my final hope was collapsing. We went back to Colmar, overcome by a disease stronger than us—stronger than love. We left Paris, relieved that our son was no longer in pain, but knowing we were taking a deadly path, the home stretch leading to the worst pain—that of nothingness and separation forever.

Chapter Ten

The Last Raspberries

I t was August 15th. A close friend of the family drove Frantz and his father back to Alsace. I had decided to make the journey alone in the small Ford Fiesta car and to follow them from afar. I needed to gather my strength, in preparation for the terrible days that would follow. I had to gather my spirits, regain control of myself, and cry profusely before pretending to be standing strong.

Those lonely days in Paris had knocked me out. Not only was I physically and mentally exhausted, but I was also completely devastated. I hadn't eaten anything in days. I remember that on my way home from the hospital I often nibbled on a few crackers I found there and lay down sobbing. Sometimes, screaming with rage, I would hit the wall with my fists as the ultimate reflex against a fight I was losing.

Late in the afternoon, we arrived at our house in Ingersheim. Life was shrinking every day, while my heart begged, pleading into the void of my non-existent spirituality: "A little more time! One more day, please!! And another and another!"

I was doing the little normal things of life when nothing was normal. We had not dared to to ask the doctor in Paris for more details about the dreaded deadline, but each of us knew. I cried at night and Jacques tenderly took me in his arms. Nothing was said; there was nothing to say. There was nothing to do either, except to continue the bond of love between the three of us.

Somehow, I do not know how, we found out about a practitioner treating cancers with alternative medicines in Colmar. The next day we were received by a strangely gentle man with a whimsical appearance suggesting a series of vitamin C shots that we categorically refused. So he talked about stars, astrology, massage and cosmic messages.

The next day, standing by the door of his room, I heard the assured and melancholic voice of my little boy, who, like the child in "The Little Prince" by Saint-Exupéry, warned me of his flight: "You know, Mom, I would like to join my star, and I do not want this doctor."

During this brief period, defying the drama, we tried to lead the most normal life possible, but everything disintegrated. As we walked through the streets of Colmar, I noticed that Frantz was no longer even interested in the window of his favorite toy store. He was moving away from us.

Although born in June, my forty years were celebrated in the middle of August, as my mother tried desperately to cheer us up. The few sips of champagne that I managed to swallow had a bitter taste and the beauty of the colors of the Hermes scarf she gave me left me completely indifferent.

For his part, Frantz, aloof to this falsely joyful distraction, and absent from life, gently withdrew. He was no longer the beautiful little boy, adventurous and joking, who despised danger, climbing rocks and scrambling up steep paths. He was no longer the impetuous little tough guy with an impatient will, the rebellious and mischievous boy. Now there was only resignation and abandonment.

Our life was shrinking more every day; we no longer went out on the street, then, no longer left the house. Finally, we no longer left our room but passed the last two days on our bed. This space became our last refuge, where more courageous than me, Jacques read in an almost cheerful voice a few passages of a comic book. The three of us never left each other and slept together, wrapped in love.

On August 24th, our little boy, in an unsure gesture, had trouble finding his mouth and his explanation pierced my heart: "Since this morning, I can hardly see anymore." His calm tone, devoid of complaint, once again demonstrated the strength of his character and perhaps also the cessation of his fight. In the room, only my voice resonated. Frantz was starting to leave us, on tiptoe...I read him stories whose meaning escaped me completely, the words coming out of my mouth automatically. My panicked heart burst out in sadness as I tried to remain normal.

Toward the end of the afternoon, Frantz looked at me intensely. Tears flowed gently from his eyes, sliding over his temples, descending along his cheeks, and pooling at his neck. He was lying on his back and I was sitting next to him, my head above his little body that could no longer bear to be sick. The tears that I could no longer control fell relentlessly on my little boy whom I had not been able to protect from the evil that was driving him away from me forever. We were at the end of the road. We both knew that everything was going to stop. The ultimate adversary was before us, hideous and terrifying. "Mom, why are we both crying?"

Braver than I, Frantz had dared to ask the real question. I did not have the courage to answer. I no longer had the strength to hold anything back and my tears flowed while my hands stroked his face, our drowned eyes united in the ultimate suffering—that of separation. In his little, calm voice, my ten-year-old boy had expressed the intensity of the desperate emotion that overwhelmed us both. I had been unable to do so. He knew and said what I had never wanted to admit. Death was there, an implacable presence, prowling around us, ready to engulf us. I was warned, but I was not ready. How could I have been? How could I be ready to give up the purest love, that of my child?

"Mom," he murmured again in a sad little voice, "we say goodbye..."

It was more of a statement than a question. The intonation of his voice revealed his awareness of the cruel and implacable reality. Frantz was going to die and I had to accept it. Frantz was dying before my eyes and I had to let him go, but to where? I had no faith in the afterlife nor hope for a better place.

The signs of his imminent departure ravaged my heart, planting there unbearable, indelible despair.

On our return from Paris, I felt compelled to get a book of medical information. I had read there that during the very last stage of leukemia, the sick became blind and that it was necessary then to treat their pain.

I refused to let my son suffer more, just as I had refused to let him die. I understood that this was the end and that we needed help.

Jacques phoned his anesthesiologist friend whose wife, head of the pediatrics department, had offered to help: a room in her hospital was at our disposal as soon as we deemed it necessary. With compassion and efficiency, this dear friend would help us at the final moment.

Then everything rushed forward.

Like every night since our return from Paris, Frantz, huddled between the two of us and ended up falling asleep, as did Jacques, defeated by exhaustion. I remained awake, alone, and replayed the moments of the day in my head. The small plate of spaghetti, which my son had asked for and the red raspberries, which he had feasted on, showing a burst of life. Even though I had to help him find the way to his mouth, he had eaten. I naively told myself, clinging to a senseless hope, that these taste pleasures still revealed a spark of life in him and not death. How could Frantz, who was dying, still have these kinds of desires? I revolted against the signs of death, illustrated by the delicate resignation of my son and his veiled gaze. I finally fell asleep with what would be the last "proofs" of life-- this light meal bringing a little smile, and the enjoyment of the red raspberries, full of life and sun.

In the middle of the night, awakened by our little boy crying in pain, we called the ambulance to go to the hospital where our friend and her team were waiting for us. Her presence and friendly help were invaluable to us.

Under the effect of morphine, Frantz no longer spoke but could possibly hear us. His breath became light, and his father and I told him that we were there with him and that we loved him. Jacques ended up dozing off in the chair near the bed, holding Frantz's hand, as he also slept peacefully.

Early in the morning, my sister and a close friend entered the room. Frantz breathed gently. He was given another dose of morphine, and his breathing became slower...I heard a very sweet sigh, and a tear flowed down his right cheek, I collected it on my finger and carried it to my lips. He was gone. It was August 25th, 1988.

Chapter Eleven

The Flight

"We love you Frantzounet, see you soon, see you soon, sweet little one," as I had called him so often…were the only words we could articulate through our tears.

It was just the three of us in the room. I closed our little boy's eyes. We were dazed, immersed in infinite sadness.

Suddenly a dove landed on the ledge of the little bedroom window, giving me a little touch of sweetness. I looked at the bird perched against the glass. I could see the beating of its heart under the gray feathers and I sadly made the comparison to that of my son.

After a while, Frantz was taken to an icy room in the hospital. We could no longer stay in the room where our son had breathed his last sigh. Indeed, life reclaims its rights, and the dead offer no more interest to the white coats, especially when it comes to a child. I found it very difficult to leave this place, where my little boy's heart had stopped beating, but I understood the tension of the nurses. Parents must not see this little dead body, revealing a medical failure as well as the finality of it all. In the twentieth century, death was concealed, and the distress that surrounded it was often hidden.

I understand this attitude, nourished by anguish and a rejection of death. At the beginning of Frantz's disease, I had the same reasoning when, one day, a mother and her child who had been given chemotherapy arrived in the hospital room in a miserable state. Selfishly, we asked to change rooms because we could no longer bear to be faced with the pain of this mother and the devastating consequences of the treatments. We wanted to be strong and fight, with the certainty of recovery. The little boy and his mother were moved elsewhere.

I still am filled with shame and regret over my selfish and unsupportive attitude, and I still envision the plight of this woman, to whom I responded with fear and flight.

★★★

A modest sheet covered the body of our little boy and the three of us went down to the basement to a refrigerated room. It was very hot outside in the summer of 1988, but this place was freezing cold and I was shaking as much with cold as with grief. Rays of sunlight filtering through the skylight above Frantz's body enveloped him in light. I put my signet ring on his finger, so he would keep something of me with him wherever he went. Jacques and I remained still for a long time, not daring to move. Sometimes we touched our son, talking to him as if he had not left us. Our tears gushed out softly, silently, from our shattered hearts.

Then a kind of fog came over me. My whole being escaped time and space, I felt I was no longer on Earth. What had happened? How did I get out of the hospital and with whom? My consciousness had left me and I remember nothing except that Frantz was transported to the Colmar morgue and that was unbearable to me.

I also don't know anything about all the paperwork that had to be completed for us to take our son's body home. I do remember that a police officer informed Jacques and my sister that a death certificate, signed by the pediatrician at the hospital, would be essential for this to be possible.

We settled our little guy in our car, stretched out in the back seat. I had a feeling of unreality and of Jacques being a robot as we drove slowly. I saw his tears fall on his knees. Nothing seemed to have changed, the road was the same, the houses too, the normal landscape unchanged. The tornado had only touched our hearts and our lives. How was it possible to live after such an upheaval? It was all over, everything collapsed on August 25th with the death of our child. Life had no meaning, no interest, no pleasure.

It was then that something extraordinary happened: a magnificent rainbow suddenly lit up the darkness of the stormy sky and surreptitiously crept into a corner of my heart. Why did a simple weather phenomenon impress me so strongly? Why was it speaking so deeply to me? Why, in all this pain was I, at this precise moment, a little reassured, as if at peace?

We arrived at the house. I don't remember what exactly happened, but I remember we laid Frantz on our bed, and we lay down next to him. Two or three days passed during which I drank a lot of whiskey and spoke deliriously to my nieces who came to visit us. In the vagueness of my memories, I remember categorically refusing the assistance of a priest, whose presence my mother would have liked. Then, at the end of this unreal time, doped by alcohol and despair, we decided to cremate our little boy. We wanted to do it privately as a couple, with no one around us, no religious people, no family, no music, no frills. Sadness in its raw state joining the purest love.

On August 28th, we were near Mulhouse, in front of the crematorium. Inside, our son was waiting to go up in smoke. We were floating in a daze as we watched the little coffin enter the place where, consumed by flames, it would emerge as only ashes. I could not walk anymore. Supported by Jacques, I went with him out onto a sort of terrace. He put his arms around me and looked up at the sky. My nose buried in my husband's chest, I was only sobs. Everything was finished. Forever separated from our little boy, I was sure I would not be able to live without him. I didn't have any fight remaining. I had no more projects, no more appetite for life; there was only the desire to die.

We went home very slowly in a silence filled with despair.

A week following the cremation, a phone call let us know that the ashes could be collected from the flower shop in front of the hospital. I went there immediately. Like a robot, I wrote the check and then was given the urn containing my child's ashes. I squeezed the burgundy pot to my chest and ran away.

Part Three: The Revelation

Chapter Twelve

Still Far from the Sky

"*I revealed myself to those who did not ask for me; I was found by those who did not seek me.*" (Isaiah 65:1)

Throughout Frantz's illness, we never thought of praying to God. He had been rejected and then forgotten for so many years that neither Jacques nor I, as we were living through the most traumatic months of our existence, ever thought of turning to him.

Still, he seemed to want to address us. Some signs from heaven appeared without our being aware of what they were. One day, for example, when Frantz was in the hospital, Jacques fell asleep at the wheel on his way to Strasbourg and only woke up to the sound of the gravel under the tires as he dangerously strayed to one side. Another time, he narrowly avoided a truck! I begged him to drive slowly and try to get some sleep before hitting the road. I told him that I could not bear to have both my son and my husband in the hospital or worse, and that I would be unable to continue the fight without him. We had always been three, united and inseparable. At that time, we were more so than ever. We had no accidents and I think it's no exaggeration to say that special protection was given to us during these journeys where both of us were racing to be with our child.

Another evening, more exhausted than usual, we decided to sleep in a hotel across from the hospital. On the nightstand was a little black book which Jacques picked up mechanically. Then opening it out of curiosity, he tersely sighed, "It's just a Bible."

What did we have to do with the Bible? We wanted our son to be healed; we wanted the nightmare to end; we wanted our life back. Religious things did not interest us directly or indirectly! We put the book down as I cried my heart out. Frantz was a few buildings away, very close to us, yet so far away, separated by leukemia and all its consequences.

Just as I had pushed away the priest wanting to enter Frantz's room, we now scorned this book in our hotel. God knocked on the door of our hearts that night, but we heard nothing. God was there, present in our suffering, but we did not know it.

I had ferociously eliminated him from my life and had such animosity toward the religion of my childhood that having our son baptized as an infant had been out of the question. This was only my view initially but Jacques readily accepted it. We both thought the baptism of our child under these conditions would be pure hypocrisy. This solemn act would then become an odious counterfeit of a belief that had long since disappeared. Both of us had never accepted the doctrine of a church imposing on its faithful a whole series of dogmas and sacraments indispensable for entering paradise. Being baptized could not be the obligatory passport to approach God, if he actually existed—which we strongly doubted at that time.

One day on his way home from school, Frantz, who knew of my aggressive opposition to religion, preferred to direct his question to his father: "Daddy, do you believe in God?" Many years have passed since our little boy, who was then about eight years old, asked this. But I remember the answer vividly, and it accurately reflected our way of living and thinking. We were in the car and Jacques let go of the steering wheel with one hand, rubbed his son's head tenderly and replied, "Right now, that's not my primary concern. Later, when I have time, I'll think about it--maybe when I retire...we have a lifetime for that..."

Although I had enrolled him in a Catholic school because of its excellent academic reputation, I had asked that our son be exempt from all religious lessons, explaining to the administration that having no faith, I did not want him to be brainwashed, as I had been in my childhood. On the contrary, I wanted him to do the research himself later and make his own decision. I wanted to give him spiritual openness and protect his free will to choose, but I didn't realize that I was actually locking him in another prison, where God was absent, and was not offering him other perspectives.

After a few weeks of religious segregation, I was warned by his school's director that Frantz was suffering from this isolation, and I immediately gave my consent for him to join Father André's classes, with whom he got along very well. Our son therefore heard about God and Jesus at that time. I suppose a lot of questions emerged in his little head. One of them, certainly important to him, concerned his parents' belief or lack of belief in the Christian God, about which he was hearing for the first time.

I loved my son too much to add to his confusion and reiterate my aversion to any form of religion. I shut my mouth and let him continue his education at the Catholic school.

When he wanted to make his first communion a year later, I explained to him that it was useless if it was just to have a party and gifts. I told him that if he did, for the sake of consistency, he would then go to mass every Sunday and do whatever the Catholic religion asks: confession, Lent, prayers, etc. I was in a good position to paint a bleak picture of Catholic rites!

Frantz chose not to make his first communion and we resumed our life, without any religiosity, leaving him to navigate alone his nascent spirituality. Our little boy, taken aback and perhaps disappointed, never asked us about God again, but he heard about Jesus once a week.

When his diagnosis stabbed us like a dagger two years later, did Frantz remember anything that had been said in his religion lessons? Did his little heart beat for Jesus, as his father's and mine had thirty years earlier? Only the Lord knows. Our spiritual closure at the time does not allow me to answer this question—something I regret today.

After Frantz's death, when well-meaning Catholics told us about purgatory, and others, much less compassionate, gave us horrified looks at the news of the unbaptized child scandal, we said to ourselves, indeed, God must be quite different since he was far above human thoughts and our narrow religious regulations.

By rejecting religious traditions, we were genuine and believed that sincerity prevailed over hypocrisy and decorum. The baptismal water droplets on our baby's head would not have protected him from his leukemia. They certainly wouldn't have given him a pass to enter Heaven. During our later spiritual research, when we read the Bible, we learned that God is Love and He vomits lukewarm followers: "I know your deeds, that you are neither cold nor hot. I wish you were either one or the other. So, because you are lukewarm—neither cold nor hot, I will spit you out of my mouth." (Revelation 3: 15-16)

Our conclusions were already affirmed by the Word of God: a heart in sincere search for the truth is better than any religiosity and since faith is a personal encounter with God, one cannot decide on it for others. The question of Frantz's non-baptism, despite our Catholic origins, gave us no guilt or remorse. We had applied what our hearts told us to, in all intellectual honesty.

After the death of our son, God, in His immense mercy, led us to seek Him with all our hearts. The path was difficult and steep, marked with obstacles. In this intense spiritual search, the grace of God was sufficient and his faithful and sure protection never failed us. We were redirected many times as we headed down various dead-end roads. We were rescued when we got bogged down in false beliefs, drawing us to futile hopes. Above all, I was prevented, at the last moment, from carrying out an irreversible plan to die.

Chapter Thirteen

Is Anyone Up There?

The trigger for our quest began about two weeks after Frantz's death. When he disappeared, I was unable to live in the big house in Ingersheim where the three of us had lived for several years. Frantz's belongings were everywhere and I could not stand the sight of them. His books, the TV, the sofa where we had curled up for endless cuddles and had watched and laughed together at Raymond Devos' jokes, the wardrobe where his clothes hung miserably, the roller skates, and his bicycle. All these things from before August 25th were given or thrown away almost immediately. I didn't want to keep anything from that happy time. Subsequently, on the occasion of a compulsory annual visit to the house to look for a few things, I avoided his room at all costs.

"Inanimate objects, do you have a soul that clings to our soul with the strength to love?", wrote Lamartine with great sensitivity.

Yes, all of these objects that had been so intimately linked to our lives were impossible to observe without a monstrous wave of sadness and despair washing over me. I couldn't accept having these things which placidly continued their quiet existences around me while my son's life had been torn from me. We decided to leave that house and set up a place between the bakery and the Croissanterie. This small room would become our refuge for more than seven years. We put in a bed and a carpet and kept Frantz's urn on a shelf with a candle. This little place to sleep and live after work would be what I quickly began calling our shoebox, the lid of which would only pop up on rare occasions. I could cry there, scream, and make all kinds of plans to end my suffering. Out of sight, I could let my sobs and cries of despair sink into the pillow and get lost in it endlessly. I could live my pain, away from those who told me to turn the page--travel and forget! Their thoughtless words demonstrated that they did not understand what we had been through, and were so harsh and devoid of compassion that we didn't want to hear them anymore. We would put the lid on our little shoebox, and after the store closed, we would not be around for anyone.

I was afraid to go out and meet people and I stubbornly refused to go to Colmar. I knew I couldn't walk where the three of us had walked or see the shops where Frantz had picked out his toys, let alone sit on the terraces where we had enjoyed a Coke. Everything broke my heart. Everything was painful. Nothing soothed my pain.

No longer having any interest in life, the idea of suicide tormented me constantly. We had no more plans, no more enthusiasm, no more momentum. We were both broken, shattered, and destroyed. I saw my husband as sad and distraught as I was, but still trying to go on. We were both survivors of a drama that I could not come to terms with. I told myself that I had to end this once and for all. I thought that with the force of life in him, Jacques would be okay without me and that my leaving would set him free in some way. All these ideas came to me without prompting and with haunting words, which like poisoned arrows slashed my mind and heart.

It was mid-September. About three weeks had passed since our little boy had gone up in smoke in the crematorium in Mulhouse. The pain of separation grew stronger every day, more oppressive too. It sapped my energy and transformed my whole being into a phantom, unable to think or act. Sometimes I wasn't quite sure where I was or what I was doing. I was nothing but tears and despair.

I was determined that I was going to part with my pain; I was going to take my life. I had found a soft and easy way. I would ingest a potent mixture of sleeping pills and alcohol and quietly walk away from this world. I would go somewhere else—a place I didn't know, but which, it seemed to me, couldn't be any worse than the current state in which I found myself.

Despite everything, I found it cowardly to leave without informing Jacques, and I also suffered from the thought of abandoning him. We had shared everything for twenty years. The wonderful times came back to me, as well as the most difficult times. I realized that, depending on the circumstances of life, we had battled, but sometimes also framed far-fetched dreams and then, together, we had created ways to make them come true. Fundamentally united and in harmony, determined to get out of difficulty, like cats, we had always known how to land on our feet.

So, I could not leave this world without informing the one who had fought like me, with all his might, and who had suffered as much as I had over the death of our son. No need to tell him about my misery since he was in similar pain. No need to tell him about the withdrawal from life since he was experiencing it too. At the start of one of those afternoons, as sad as the day before, but certainly not as hopeless as the next day would be, I decided to talk to him and describe my plans and how I was going to execute them.

I can still see very clearly his expression of immeasurable sadness, mixed with a perfect understanding of what I was going through and his deep love for me as well. He stood up slowly and pulled me against him with infinite tenderness. His voice, heavy with emotion and sorrow, softly whispered the phrases that were certainly inspired in him, and which changed my destiny and his.

"Ariane, I understand you, I can't take it anymore either. But do you think this is the best way to find Frantz? He was so brave during his illness, our little guy, shouldn't we be as brave as he was? He showed us by example."

Our tears mingled as he spoke of those six months of struggle and dashed hopes. I stopped crying. I understood what he meant to say: Where was my courage? Where was my will? I fell silent. The three of us had lost the horrific battle with leukemia. Was there now another battle to be fought? I shut up.

After a few minutes, Jacques gently released me and, his voice now assured, added the words which troubled my mind and my heart: "I believe we should do spiritual research and find out if there is life after death. If we don't find anything credible, then I'll let you take your life, and maybe I will too."

The rationality of those two sentences, so simple and so logical, struck me deeply. Through Jacques' mouth, the divine breath rekindled in me a small flame of spirituality, suggesting that I seek the Creator of this breath and thereby the meaning of life.

I accepted Jacques' offer.

Chapter Fourteen

Maybe

That's when the most extraordinary adventure of our lives began: the adventure that led to the Light. The story of an encounter. The Father's love story, welcoming with open arms, a prodigal son and daughter. In short, a simple family story.

As you read this account, you may discover absolute love or marvel at God's stubborn determination to save his creatures and his loving tenacity in creating opportunities to reveal himself.

As in the Old Testament, with the people of Israel in the wilderness, God moved us forward according to his guidance and our inclination to listen to him.

We were guided by signs and information that our hearts still saw as chance. This scripture passage reminds us of our own journey under the protection of the Lord and the inspiration of the Holy Spirit:

"In all the travels of the Israelites, whenever the cloud lifted from above the tabernacle, they would set out; but if the cloud did not lift, they did not set out—until the day it lifted. So the cloud of the Lord was over the tabernacle by day, and fire was in the cloud by night, in the sight of all the Israelites during all their travels." (Exodus 40: 36-38)

We were nurtured, supported, and protected by the providence of an omniscient God who knew the desperate quest of our hearts: to find Frantz's love, by any means possible. By inquiring about the possibility of a future with our little boy, we were unconsciously looking for God since he is Love. Our approach corresponded perfectly to the phrase of the prophet Isaiah: *"Before they call on me, I will answer; before they are done speaking, I will hear."* (Isaiah 65:24)

We saw discreet and dazzling signs of the Father's tenderness, which we experienced simultaneously or sometimes separately. We had dazzling moments together, moments when the truth imposed itself with calm firmness. We were never coerced or manipulated, but treated as responsible adults with free will.

At first, we were not yet ready to admit that the only real God was the one revealed by Jesus Christ, whose incarnation, death, and resurrection were announced in the New Testament.

Our spiritual search was strewn with struggles, mistakes, and trial and error. God, respecting our choices, left us free to take side roads and to make frequent mistakes. Dangerous stalemates or near-fatal falls were nothing new to us.

"Ask, and it will be given to you; seek, and you will find; knock, and it will be opened to you." (Matthew 7:7) Yes, but you have to knock on the right door—and find the right person!

Shortly after Frantz's death, when I did not want to leave "the shoebox" for any reason, I had the absurd idea of going to a garage that also functioned as a grocery store. I remember my confused reaction amid the hubbub. I was a little dazed by so much activity and had no specific goal. I wondered about my coming to this place and what I should buy. Scanning the shelves, I told myself that Jacques would gladly eat a piece of cheese and like a sleepwalker, I grabbed the first one within reach. At the checkout, noticing a newspaper rack, I mechanically grabbed a *Paris Match* and returned home. "But why did I buy these things?" I asked Jacques, who was as surprised as I was.

The weekly tabloid remained closed for several days because neither Jacques nor I were interested in the romantic adventures of the celebrities of the moment or in the highly publicized life of Caroline of Monaco. That kind of futile news, which sometimes distracted us before, was totally irrelevant in the face of the drama we were living. We had become like hermits, completely indifferent to the gossip of the world.

One afternoon, while Jacques was recuperating from his night's work, I leafed through the magazine without interest, wondering once again what had possessed me to buy it. On the very last page, my eye was caught by the header of an article titled "Life After Death?" It spoke of a Belgian journalist's book, *The Dark Source* (Patrick Van Eersel, *La Source noire,* Paris: Grasset, 1986).

According to the information and serious investigations collected over several years, this journalist explained that it was not unreasonable to ponder a possible form of life after death. I excitedly read and re-read his conclusions and had Jacques read the article as soon as he awoke. We agreed that we needed this book immediately! So we started investigating the hottest topic in the world: Is there really life after life? We knew that our future depended on the answer. Mine in particular was in jeopardy, but I didn't forget Jacques's critical sentence: "If we don't find anything serious, then I'll let you kill yourself and maybe I will too."

The author had conducted extensive research on the question of the afterlife, interviewing doctors, scientists, clerics, and people who had undergone what are called near-death experiences. These adults and children, declared clinically dead after an accident or an illness, recounted their experiences during the few moments they were on the other side. Their motionless journey had often led them to encounter a bright light and to feel a great peace, which they all described as supernatural.

Jacques and I feverishly read their testimonies and had no doubts about the honesty of their stories. We dwelt on the passages speaking of well-being, joy, and the total removal of the dread of death upon their return to life. Although these witnesses did not know each other, their descriptions overlapped and in many cases were practically the same, which gave them a serious ring of authenticity.

We were on a path, but we wanted to dig much further, much deeper. These stories did us good and convinced us that the search would be long. We knew that we had to abandon the pitfalls of Cartesian reasoning and primary logic, which limit human thought far too much. We had to open ourselves to the "possible", to the "why not," and let ourselves try other ways of thinking.

We bought all the books referenced by the writer of *The Dark Source*. Those of Dr. Elisabeth Kubler-Ross struck us and particularly moved us. She had done much interesting research and had concluded that we have an afterlife. Without any religious philosophy at the beginning of her work, but endowed with an honest professional conscience, this Swiss doctor helped us to accept the idea of a form of life in the afterlife.

Her conversations with little leukemia patients echoed our pain. It seemed to us that the accounts of children who had near-death experiences could not be forged. We believed in the sincerity of these little beings who were not manipulated for media or religious purposes. The doctor told the story of these children at the end of life, with great compassion and tenderness, but she also did not omit the observed and meticulously recorded medical details.

We were often in tears, but we welcomed with a certain relief the spark of hope offered by the possibility of an afterlife. We now had a clear goal, and there was no question of giving up until we knew. We were therefore engulfed in this luminous gap, though the outcome was uncertain. We needed a lot of documentation. We had to read and learn about everything going on in the scientific and medical world dealing with this issue. Some were serious and very precise and if they did not absolutely confirm life after death, they insisted on its possibility.

But conversely, many works turned out to be completely insane. Indeed, unscrupulous people shamefully took advantage of the distress of the bereaved by publishing literature as implausible as it was misleading. Some promised contact with the dead, others said they heard their voices, not to mention those who claimed they could make them appear. Some spiritualists worked with a photo of the dead and shamelessly asked to add to their consequent bill a garment or a fabric having belonged to the disappeared. Some claimed to receive words addressed to families, while others deciphered coded messages coming straight from the sky.

A few years earlier, when he was still single and living a bohemian life, Jacques, who was attracted to the Tibetan religion, which he often talked about with his karate friends, had an original experience, to say the least. Scrupulously following the advice of the Tibetan monk Lobsang Rampa, his mind began what is called in transcendental meditation an "out of body experience." But he was seized with such panic when the bed moved and his body stirred that he quickly put an end to the adventure. The description he gave me of the details of that evening gave him shivers of anguish and unease for a long time afterward.

We had both experimented with occult practices in the past, and they often seemed to work. For my part, I was attracted by fortune tellers whose series of truths had proven their supernatural power to me. Jacques and I had even seen tables move during spiritualism sessions where we invoked the spirits through an Ouija board and were given disturbing answers, to say the least.

Finally, a random customer from the Croissanterie, looking at the palm of my hand, and with tears in his eyes predicted, in veiled language, the death of my son, who at that time was in perfect health. I did not understand his strange look and his mysterious words until years later, after Frantz was gone.

We could not deny the existence of a parallel world, while we still disputed the very existence of God!

Chapter Fifteen

The Gimmick

Raoul, a Belgian living in Colmar, was very focused on esoteric subjects and was a regular at the Croissanterie. He provided us with New Age books and all kinds of literature dealing with occult sciences. This man in his fifties was part of a sect claiming to cure diseases through selective food. According to him, their patients regained their health through baths and massages as well as by the absorption of raw foods, chosen according to their tastes and instincts. This method was called instinctotherapy. His companion had once been part of the cult, the Children of God, and continued to believe in all kinds of obscure ideas. The couple came regularly to the Croissanterie and we developed a friendship. Despite my pain, with what little humor I had left, I wondered if I, who loved chocolate so much, could have cured my fragile liver by the daily absorption of a large quantity of that delicious dark confectionery!

As desperate as we were, we still could not accept this religious-culinary farce.

Raoul and others had been supplying us with various works of this kind for a few months now and we had accumulated around fifty books and treatises. Some asserted the existence of a "life after life" by describing their paranormal experiences of communication with the deceased, while others spoke of reincarnation and karma. None of this seemed acceptable to us and we were in shock at the prospect of our baby boy being reborn as a fly or a cow! The writings of the "New Age" religious movement also seemed to us to lack any real basis and left us perplexed. Their current of thought cheerfully mixed the doctrines of several religions and

Eastern philosophies with a few verses from the Christian Gospel distilled in homeopathic doses. This mystical melting pot could not satisfy our thirst for truth, and we felt that these spiritual appetizers did not meet our needs. We demanded the Truth, the only value that could help us survive. Otherwise, I was determined to go and see for myself the other side of the veil.

We sometimes came across Protestant authors who were difficult to read for the neophytes that we were, because their biblical quotations did not speak to us. Unable to grasp the fullness of Christ's reality, we were nevertheless happy to find some hope of resurrection there. Disenchanted, I closed these books with a long sigh. I was not ready to accept what I had flat-out refused for over thirty years!

We continued for long months looking in all directions for an answer to our nagging need to find something coherent. One autumn afternoon, as our investigations stalled, a friendly man walked into the bakery and quickly struck up a conversation with me. Had he seen the look in my sad eyes and felt my distress and questioning? Was he clairvoyant? Indeed, he spoke to me of the possibility of contacting the dead very easily. There was an association in Colmar whose purpose was to establish a connection with people from the other world. And, he announced with a mysterious smile, a meeting was to be held that very evening at a place nearby.

Then he added in a low voice, "I would be very happy to welcome you there because there is always something special going on in these meetings." Then, with a stare, he reiterated his invitation just before walking out the door: "In your state, it would do you the greatest good!"

Isolated and desperate as we were, we were easy prey. Moreover, having already lost everything, we had nothing more to fear, and so we decided to go.

When we arrived, the big room with large windows filled up quickly, and everyone seemed to know each other. The wait for the master lasted only a few minutes; then in respectful silence, he entered. The session began immediately with all sorts of incantations that the man in black recited in a deep voice. On the table in front of him, a few books with mysterious titles attracted the curiosity of the audience, while a basket awaited donations.

After the various announcements, we were invited to sit on the floor and a regular attendee closed the curtains: the serious things were about to begin! The officials and informed spiritualists began to name the names of the dead they wanted to bring and encouraged newcomers to say the names of their deceased. The tone rose, peppered with shrill cries as the evening progressed. A few candles placed here and there gave off a gloomy light, revealing the haggard faces of our neighbors. Everyone seemed to be in the grip of panic and extreme nervous tension in this heavy atmosphere. After about fifteen minutes, hoots from all corners of the room gave us goosebumps. This collective trance of a hundred people suddenly plunged us into total bewilderment and fear. And when guttural voices roared, declaring that they saw the dead whose names had been mentioned, it was the height of horror.

"They're there! They're there!" a voice cried.

"I see them! I see them!" shouted another.

"They're on horses!" yelled a third.

"They're coming on their horses of fire! I see them, I see them, they're all here!" repeated other voices.

At the beginning of the session, we too had whispered the name of our little boy. I grabbed Jacques' hand and hoped Frantz would appear without really believing he would. But I realized now that we had been misguided. This nightmarish and hideous session of spiritualism was going nowhere.

On Saturday evening, after the store closed, Jacques bought two bottles of crémant which we drank together straight away. Then, exhausted with fatigue and alcohol, we slept like brutes practically until Monday morning. Paradoxically, the sixteen-hour work days helped us to hold on and not sink completely. Despite everything, I am grateful for this period of extremely hard work and for the customers who, without knowing it, were instrumental in our survival.

Each day passed darker than the last. I was not getting used to Frantz's absence, as I had been cruelly advised that I would by some. I could not live with my grief and had very little control over it. Since we had not found anything, I thought again about ending it all.

Chapter Sixteen

The Precious Book

R eading all that happened during this period and the events that would unfold afterward, I am convinced that God was actively present in our distressed lives. We experienced the intervention of envoys from the Kingdom, those diligent and wonderful angels, who accomplished their mission with the poor losers we had become. From this time of intense darkness, memories come to mind, a few flashes of light illuminating the actions of a God who acted with precision and love.

One afternoon, while I placed my head in the gas oven and began to breathe in the deadly gas, the sound of the door interrupted my fatal plan. A stranger with a soft and persuasive smile entered: Elisabeth. A devout Catholic with a solid faith, this parishioner had heard of the tragedy we were living.

Her genuine compassion made her find the words we needed in those days. We learned later that she had begun to intercede for us in her prayer group and in her family long before she dared approach us. Calmed by her kindness, we became friends. She accepted my mood swings, my despair, and my anger. Perfectly respecting our way of thinking and knowing that we were very much against religion, Elisabeth walked on tiptoe, not daring to go too far down the slippery slope of faith. In no way did she want to shock or repel us with overtly Christian language. Her firm assurance in the values of the Gospel sometimes annoyed us and impressed us at the same time. Animated by the tenderness of the Father, this lady was for us the first true witness of God's love.

Another illuminating time was the meeting with a Franciscan priest from Elisabeth's parish. This outspoken man with a thunderous laugh, resembled Francis of Assisi and immediately appealed to us. He had enough patience to respond calmly to our aggressive questions and our rage that swept around him like a tornado. He often came by in the afternoon and we talked while Jacques slept. He had had serious problems with the hierarchy in his ecclesiastical career and understood my hostility against the religious establishment.

He seemed a bit brutish to me in his way of being, but his deep humanity was real, and I liked him despite the spiritual distance that separated us. Because he was good, honest, and sensitive and never tried to force us into anything, we respected him. Not being ready to return to God, there was no question of returning to the Church, and his friendly visits were not sufficient to convince us of God's existence.

One morning in June, our friend Elisabeth delicately suggested that we think about taking a rest. When we reflexively objected, she added: "You are disoriented at work, you need calm and—meditation."

This idea seemed absurd to us: we lived hidden in our box and hardly ever came out. Vacation time seemed to me as unattractive as it was unreal. I didn't want to meet people, I was afraid of their questions and their behavior towards me. I was a mother without children, a mother whose son was somewhere else. To say he was dead choked me up, to say that I had no children battered my heart.

I still had in mind the dreadful memory of the visit of a mother whose children were in the same school as Frantz and who addressed me thoughtlessly: "I came to see you to find out what it's like to lose a child."

A knife stab could not have wounded me more. People have no idea what harm their careless words impose. Whether it was the talk of a jaded psychologist with cold professional curiosity or just an insensitive question thrown in my face, I was sadly bewildered by so much lack of consideration and compassion.

I didn't want to meet these kinds of people anymore, I wanted to stay protected and not suffer what my common sense urged me to avoid. My reasoning was sound, I refused to enter a hostile world as the woman I had become. I didn't have the emotional capacity to hear the sentence that hurt us so much: "We must turn the page." I had heard those painfully penetrating words too many times.

Jacques and I talked about Elisabeth's advice, and we both finally admitted we were badly in need of rest. Of course, we couldn't go to a resort or any hotel, where we would not be able to bear the sight of happy people and children playing. We were unable to endure such torture, even though we sincerely wished everyone happiness, especially parents.

It had been nine months since we had suffered the shock and trauma of our own child's death and the mere sight of a ten-year-old boy was very difficult to handle without bursting into tears. Only very sensitive people or bereaved parents could understand. The others were to be avoided. That was why I didn't want to leave.

A determined Christian, Elisabeth knew that we needed to meet Christ, in person. He alone would have the power to comfort us. It was not about seeing psychologists. Though such people were certainly able to understand us and offer tools for survival, they would prove powerless in giving us a glimmer of hope for eternal life, if they did not have faith in Jesus, the Risen One. Diplomas were useless, only the grace of God would satisfy.

As she left that morning, Elisabeth asked us to consider her proposal for a possible spiritual retreat. The following week we chose the Benedictine monastery, located in Hautecombe, in Savoy. Why did we opt for this high place of the Catholic faith where the leaders of charismatic groups from all over France came to recharge their batteries? Why did we agree to go there? Some choices are instinctive, others are considered, and then, some are brought about by those who are inspired by the Holy Spirit. We think Hautecombe was one of them.

We arrived on the shores of Lake Annecy in the middle of July. One of the reasons we had chosen this place was that we were convinced that the monastery would be isolated and immersed in nature which suited the hermits that we had become. So we were amazed to see hundreds of cars parked along the small mountain road leading to the monastery. I wanted to turn back. I felt extreme stage fright, which prevented me from breathing, and I already regretted straying from the comfort of my "shoebox."

Elisabeth had recommended that we meet the monk Marc-Francois Lacan, a friend of her family and brother of the famous psychoanalyst, Jacques Lacan. We had reserved our room at the convent, yet neither Jacques nor I wanted to continue on our way. Despite this, as we arrived at the top, Jacques defiantly broke through the heavy silence of the car: "If this monk doesn't tell us what we want to hear, we'll get the hell out of here!"

We so needed to find the certainty of the existence of God and of eternal life, and to have the assurance that we were on the right path to find our son one day. So I kept quiet and left it to Jacques to drive the car and our fate.

We entered the courtyard of the convent timidly, not yet knowing that a source of light was just waiting around the corner. The first contact with Father Marc-Francois Lacan was and will remain an unforgettable moment. This Benedictine monk, recognized by his peers as a leader in the Catholic intellectual world, welcomed us warmly. I remember his arrival in the room where Anne-Marie, the smiling hotel manager, had placed us. Sitting on the bed, crying as always, not knowing what to do or what to think, I saw the door open on a little gentleman, about eighty years old, whose spine could no longer hold his skeleton straight. He approached us quietly, a discreet smile full of kindness on his face:

"You are Jacques and Ariane; I was expecting you, and I have been informed of your arrival."

Then in a very soft voice, he suggested that we rest and offered to talk to us the next morning. Then, giving me a look full of tender compassion, without a word, he sat down on the bed, took my tear-soaked hand and whispered, "See you tomorrow; try to relax now because you've had a long trip from Alsace. See you tomorrow…"

Then he left without a sound, leaving in the room the imprint of the love of Christ. In each other's arms, we cried for a long time before going to the dining hall, a bright and soothing place. Every day, we had an appointment with Father Lacan and asked him the questions essential to our spiritual search. Never was this man of God impatient with our sometimes brutal and suspicious interrogation. Always listening to our distress and the rumbling revolt, he understood my torrents of tears and accepted Jacques' aggressive questions. Although he had a very busy schedule, we spent two hours with him every morning. This great Bible scholar, insightful intellectual, and author of many books, was also the one to whom the leaders of Catholic charismatic groups turned for advice and guidance. Father Marc-Francois Lacan was very much in demand and very busy. When we found out that his days and nights were also interrupted, every four hours, for times of prayer with his fellow monks in the chapel, we said to ourselves that we were truly privileged to spend so much time with him.

As we had conversations with him and with other monks, we felt our souls gradually opening up to the love of God. The story of the prodigal son completed the softening of our hearts, and we were now ready to renew contact with the One who had never left us.

We went to the chapel in the afternoon and while the monks chanted their magnificent Gregorian chants, we began to pray again. We invoked the saints and the Virgin Mary and prayed to Jesus with all our hearts, with the faith of rediscovered childhood. When, at the end of the stay, in our logic as former Catholics, we asked to confess, Father Lacan, with a smile as indulgent as he was amused, said something we would never forget: "There is no rush my children! That will be for later; that's not the most important! What you need now is to read the Word of God—buy a Bible!" And with benevolent authority, he directed us to the convent bookstore where, at the age of forty, we bought our first Bible.

The next day, the day of our departure, Father Lacan gave us an appointment at 4:00 a.m. in front of the door of the chapel where, during this brief stay, we had knelt so many times. He embraced us affectionately and commended us to God. Jacques then asked him to bless our new Bible. How surprised we were once again, when, bursting into laughter, this knowledgeable theologian answered us with a mischievous gleam in his eye: "How do you expect me to bless the Bible! It's the Word of God! It *is* the Blessing!"

Seizing the pen from the hand of Jacques, inspired by the Holy Spirit, the man of God wrote on the first page of our Bible, Luke 10:41,42, *"Martha, Martha you worry and fuss over a lot of things. Only one is needed. Mary has chosen what is better, which will not be taken from her."* In the morning twilight, these words of the Lord hit us right in the heart, showing us the way to find God.

He urged us to follow Christ and meditate on his teachings, without encumbering ourselves with the frills. We left Hautecombe, different from when we arrived. We had rediscovered the treasure of God buried for many years under a mass of weeds and mud. In this monastery, we had tasted a little of the tenderness of God. Now we had the most effective aid in the world to help us go on living. The Bible would become our life reference, and with prayer, it would be our best asset to continue to seek the Truth.

The precious book in hand, we set off again for Alsace, and from that day on, despite the many storms and obstacles still ahead, our lives were never the same. Guided by the word of God, we had now tiptoed to the edge of the kingdom of God.

Chapter Seventeen

An Unexpected Gift

W hen we were invited one day to make a pilgrimage to Medjugorje, a small village in Bosnia-Herzegovina where the Virgin was supposed to have appeared, we signed up immediately. We so wanted to receive something special from God! Our need to be connected to Heaven and to touch the beyond was inextinguishable.

The first morning, we joined the crowd of adorers of Mary and I mingled with the faithful who, shoes in hand, plodded painfully over the sharp stones and brambles of the path. I thought I would be closer to the Lord and my son by suffering like this. My feet were bleeding profusely, and the pain of every step echoed through my body as my light spirit soared to Heaven. Some demonstrations of hysteria seized the pilgrims and when we saw a young girl who was possessed, we realized that if God existed, the devil was certainly not just a myth! We heard wolf howls. Some who were accustomed to the place knelt down and began to pray feverishly, invoking God and all the saints of paradise. The guttural howls grew louder as we got closer to the top. It was terrifying and, paralyzed by what seemed to be a paranormal phenomenon, we had goosebumps.

Indeed we witnessed a scene worthy of a horror movie! A young Italian girl seized with convulsions, writhing on the ground like a snake. Her rolled-back eyes showed only white, and from her wide-open mouth came a hoarse male voice belching the names of Jesus and Mary, in words so obscene that no Italian would translate them. It was frightening and unreal at the same time, but the organizer of the trip explained to us that it happened from time to time and that exorcisers were on their way to take care of the young girl. On the way back, no longer even feeling the pain of my scratched feet, and holding Jacques's hand, I ran down the hill to return to the hotel.

In the course of this trip, I received a precious gift from the Lord. It came through the celebrant of a mass without his knowledge, during a stop on the road leading to Medjugorje. Since the death of Frantz, a distressing question often came to torment me. I wondered if it was because of my many sins that my little boy had died. I felt guilty about my past life and accepted the idea of punishment from God. Remorse overwhelmed me. Perhaps a more righteous life would have saved our son from suffering and dying. It was terribly painful to think that way, but I couldn't get rid of that accusatory feeling. I often talked about it with Jacques, who didn't agree with me, but unfortunately didn't have enough solid arguments to make me change my mind.

So when, in that cold little church, the priest gave his homily from the gospel of John chapter 9, and quoted the first four verses, summing up my own questions so well, I burst into tears:

"As Jesus went along, he saw a man blind from birth. His disciples asked him, 'Rabbi, who sinned, this man or his parents, that he was born blind?' 'Neither this man nor his parents sinned,' said Jesus, 'but this happened so that the works of God might be displayed in him.'" (John 9:1-3)

I was speechless before the kindness of the Lord, who reassured me once and for all. That day, the Master took charge of my burden and shattered any form of guilt that hindered my walk toward him. Since God was alive and spoke to us through the Bible, we had good reason to hope and to continue our research in the Christian world and wherever the Word was declared. Although we certainly did not see the virgin or experience transcendent states, we did receive much from the Lord. Our earnest prayers were rewarded with greater faith and a real passion for God, as the Holy Spirit moved us to greater intimacy with the Lord Jesus. The famous place dedicated to Mary remained on our spiritual path as the place where we experienced the grace of God.

While later we were gently mocked for this pilgrimage by our Protestant friends or even harshly criticized by the most intransigent, we understood that God looks at the sincerity of hearts: *"The Lord does not look at the things man looks at. Man looks at the outward appearance, but the Lord looks at the heart."* (1 Samuel 16:7).

We had now come to understand that God was Love and therefore He forgave us for our years of wandering. As in the painting of the Prodigal Son by Rembrandt, a replica of which we had admired at the monastery of Hautecombe, we recognized God to be the Father of the prodigal son and the One who had opened his arms to us. He was no longer the monstrous Godfather of our childhood. There seemed to be the possibility of forgiveness and renewal. These perspectives gave us the desire to reconnect with the Catholic Church of our youth. We felt that the denomination of a church was not the most important thing, but, rather, that the essence of the church's spiritual life was anchored in a true relationship with the Most High.

After more than thirty years of absence, we therefore returned to Sunday masses. Kneeling in the cathedral of Colmar, we each invoked the forgiveness of the Lord, speaking to him as to a father. The ceremonial services plunged me back into the atmosphere of my childhood when my still pure heart had given itself to Jesus. I also liked the possibility of sitting on a pew in the darkness of a church, without anyone noticing me. Jacques, patient and certainly as moved as I was, waited for me to finish this heart-to-heart with God. I found it hard to leave this atmosphere where the air smelled of incense and where an inexpressible peace descended.

In these intimate moments, my soul flew up to heaven and I spoke to God about my son and to my son about God. I felt soothed in a moist cocoon of tears and love mixed together. When we finally left this reassuring darkness, the harsh light outside and the noise and the bustle of the world abruptly reminded me of the reality of life.

On Sundays, after mass, we looked for a restaurant where I would drink more than necessary to anesthetize my weariness with life. Then we would go to bed in our shelter and sleep until it was time to go to work. At that time, my anger was terrible, sweeping away and breaking everything in its path. It was never directed against God, the great outcast of my life, who I was beginning to approach once again. Nor was it directed at the doctors who had failed to cure my son. Although I would have appreciated a little more compassion from the medical profession, I had no grudge against them. The uncontrollable whirlwinds of fury, which sometimes invaded my whole being, were not against Jacques, even if my poor husband had a hard time helping me. I guess they came from a wave of immense sadness and my inability to deal with it. I think they also resulted from the enemy knowing one of my weaknesses and using it against me and our marriage.

We were two survivors, clinging to the same plank, and although we began to read the Bible and pray regularly, things were not any easier. I still wasn't getting used to Frantz's absence, and I was living his death so repeatedly that I still regularly thought about suicide.

Luc, the Franciscan priest, and Elisabeth patiently continued to visit us. Having noted our sincere desire to find God since our return from Hautecombe, Luc prayed with us and sometimes brought us communion, which all three of us took with emotion. We had received a rosary from one of the monks at the monastery, and Jacques used it at night in the bakery. When I saw him on his knees on the floor covered with flour, I smiled at the thought of Jesus who, wanting to feed the crowds of Palestine, might have asked him to prepare some rolls to accompany the fish. For my part, I lit a candle near the picture of Frantz and recited my rosary. Then I prayed and spoke to my son. We had become very Catholic!

Chapter Eighteen

A Wink of the Eye from Up High

O n the path of faith, we naturally reconnected with the church, respecting its rites and traditions. But we did not give up on expanding our spiritual horizons or continuing our journey. We cried out to the Lord for signs and tangible help. We asked Him for proof of our little boy's life. We urged God, the creator of all life, to alleviate the deep pain left by our son's death by assuring us of his existence elsewhere.

It was a lot to ask, but not too much to ask.

And in his immense love, God answered. We had signs and comfort. Then, the conviction that Frantz could not have just disappeared forever quietly settled in our hearts.

One night, a particularly desperate Jacques, came out of the bakehouse abruptly and defiantly peering up at the sky, urged God to give him a manifestation from beyond. Instantly, a dazzling star took an implausibly long time to cross the entire firmament. As if to let us admire its radiant beauty, the nocturnal star traveled nonchalantly to the other side of the night sky. Jacques was convinced that he had received a genuine answer to his aggressive question, "Is anyone up there?" The certainty that this star was not ordinary, but that it represented a sign from the God of Heaven, was a great comfort to him.

Only a few days after Frantz died, and although I still did not believe in God, I also received a signal of the existence of the Kingdom. That night, more pitiful than ever, throwing myself on the bed, I buried my head in the pillow and screamed my pain into it. Finally, drowned in my sobs, I fell asleep holding Frantz's picture. I don't know how long it took before I saw my little boy.

He walked on a large white field so brilliant I couldn't stare at him. It was dazzling with an exceptionally sparkling light. Then I heard his crystalline laughter radiating unspeakable joy, and I knew he was alive and happy where he was.

Was it a dream driven by my desire or a vision triggered from beyond? We never knew. Yet we were certain that the signs were to be taken as gifts from God. The Eternal Father was helping us to find him and come to terms with the death of our child.

It was then that we remembered the poem, "Footprints in the Sand," (origin disputed), evoking a man walking on the sand. The traveler expressed great dismay at the suffering he had endured and asked God where he was at those times. Indeed, four footprints demonstrated the presence of God at the side of the suffering man, until there were only two left, leading him to believe he was alone and abandoned. He then questioned the Lord, whose answer encouraged us immensely: "At those times, I was carrying you!"

We wondered, was the Lord honoring the commitment we made when we were little? Did he grant our wish to follow him because, in his omniscience, he knew of our turnaround? Or was he simply God, merciful and full of love for the children that we were and that, for Him, we had never ceased to be? Unable to fathom his thoughts, we could only experience his love and receive his Grace. But what were we to do with it all? We were not Abraham, to whom God had said: *"Shall I hide from Abraham what I am about to do?"* (Genesis 18:17). We were only Jacques and Ariane stuck in the drama that had led us on this spiritual quest, bringing us back, after thirty years of absence, to the embrace of the Father.

Our enthusiasm to rediscover him became insatiable, and our fervor somehow overcame our bitter regrets. Sunday Masses, with immutable routines and weak biblical teaching, frustrated our hunger for the Holy Scriptures. After such a long interval, our souls could not be satisfied with a lukewarm homily, more like a social discourse than a spiritual appeal. We wanted solid, authentic, and verifiable truths from the Bible.

In Alsace, the Christian communities have not been torn apart, and joint prayer meetings between Catholics and Protestants are organized regularly. That was certainly an additional asset in our spiritual journey. We ran to every meeting advertised by Christians of all denominations. It didn't matter to us whether they were Catholic or Protestant, the important thing was that we prayed there together to the God of the Bible. We felt we were on the right path and wanted to continue to learn and progress toward the One whom we believed was the only one who could bring us peace. We did not think then that he was even capable of giving meaning to our lives and thereby a new joy...

★★★

We were more and more attracted by the rigor of Protestant teaching and their knowledge of the Bible, and we drank up every teaching given by pastors in the prayer meetings. The verses jumped out at us then, because they answered in a precise way the questions that we had asked ourselves a few days before. The Holy Spirit was working in us and helping us understand a little about God's plan.

It was also during this period that the phrase of the philosopher Edith Stein imposed itself on us: "God is Truth, whoever seeks truth, seeks God, whether he realizes it or not." We had to strive for our goal: to seek the essential truths with all our might and feed on God's words.

One day, I happened to read a local newspaper ad from a lady bragging about her ability to communicate with spirits and her experience in contacting those in the afterlife. She boasted of a 90% success rate and promised clear conversations with the dead. Drawn like a magnet to a piece of metal and unable to take my eyes off the eloquent advertisement, I picked up the phone and made an appointment.

The day passed as usual, and at the end of the afternoon, we had an unexpected visit. Our notary clerk pushed open the door with an embarrassed smile. Showing great delicacy, this woman whom we barely knew, murmured a few words of condolence and asked me to sign some administrative papers. I walked her to her car, which I didn't usually do. Saying goodbye, she handed me a flyer that despite the pouring rain, had stuck to her windshield wipers from the center of Colmar: "Do you mind putting this in the trash?" I absently grabbed the printout, went back into the shop, and put it on the table next to the medium's announcement.

When I was going to bed I saw this green flier, which, despite the long journey and the rain, was still in good condition and on which I read, amazed, the following Bible verse: *"Do not turn to mediums or seek out spiritists, for you will be defiled by them. I am the Lord your God,"* (Leviticus 19:31).

I was in shock! No one except the spiritualist and I knew my intentions. Jacques was sleeping innocently in the next room, not knowing what was going on on the other side of the door. I grabbed the Bible we had bought in Hautecombe and searched feverishly for the quoted passages. Then, proof in front of me, shivering and amazed, I realized that not only was the God of the Bible the true God, but He knew me and knew what I was going to do and was warning me by his Word of imminent danger.

A wave of gratitude and emotion washed over me. My tears flowed in torrents, but for the first time since Frantz's death, they were not the expression of infinite sadness. On the contrary, they were tears of new joy in the face of God's intervention to protect me.

Chapter Nineteen

The Guardian Angels

Our progress, punctuated by many questions, remained fragile despite the excitement of having discovered a treasure. We had allowed ourselves to be found by the Lord, but that was not enough to satisfy our spiritual ambition. It caused us to delve more deeply into the heart of God. We wanted to know him more and submit to him completely. Perhaps the passionate enthusiasm for the discovery of the Almighty called for a more radical attitude, and our search required a concrete step on our part: an important piece of the puzzle was missing.

One day we met a woman and her adopted son who befriended us. Very involved in the Catholic Church, this nice retiree tried to support us by attentive and friendly listening. We greatly appreciated her smile, friendliness, and practical help in times of great distress. She knew all the lively spiritual groups in the region and suggested that we spend a Sunday in a community on the other side of the Vosges. Speculating that we could start another life there, she insisted that we become members of this group because, strong in her Christian psychology, she assured us categorically: "This is what you need!"

It is true that for some time, we had wondered what we should do with this new life of which God was henceforth the pilot, and how we could serve him. Our passion for the Lord had created a real need to communicate our newfound faith to the world. Jacques, especially, was inexhaustible in sharing our newfound relationship with God. We had to find a place where we could give free rein to the exuberance of our hearts. We had come so far and had to make up for so much lost time!

Getting to know several charismatic communities prompted some interesting experiences but did not convince us to join any of them. For some, their secluded and self-sufficient way of life, their repressive rules, and their assurance of holding the truth did not correspond to our independent personalities and free spirits. It did not seem pleasant or judicious to us to put ourselves under guardianship.

Our septuagenarian friend, disappointed and perhaps offended by our categorical refusal, visited less and less often, then never returned. Again, we were off and did not fulfill the expectations of normal people. I felt more misunderstood and marginalized than ever, and I felt a great nostalgia for my life before the tragedy.

The goal of our spiritual inquiry had been achieved: we were reassured about the afterlife, and we knew God. But there was the inevitable question of our future—what would we do about our faith? What would we do with our faith? What was the missing link?

Our need for human warmth, solidarity and compassion was deep. My mother called me from time to time from Paris and burst into tears with me. These shared sobs hurt me, but at the same time brought me the comfort of knowing that someone else was grieving over the death of my little one, and was neither ashamed nor afraid to express it. I think the worst attitude towards parents who have lost a child is silence and denial of the suffering endured. Pretending to believe that life goes on as before adds unbearable pain to that already experienced every day.

"When the child appears, the family circle applauds loudly," writes Victor Hugo. In the case of the death of a child, the sentence becomes very different because the loved ones, unable to cope with the tragedy, flee most of the time, leaving a deafening silence.

My hysterical crying and my anger had not disappeared, and Jacques had a hard time managing these tornadoes sweeping away everything in their path. Having become a Christian, he reached for help from on High. When I was screaming so much that I lost my voice and was smashing everything within my reach, Jacques could now speak to the One who had authority over the storms. He knew that only the Lord was capable of the miracle of quieting the tsunami that he alone could not master. *"What kind of man is this? Even the winds and the waves obey him!"* (Matthew 8:27)

And then the miracle happened: the door opened on one of the only two people who could help us.

First, Lucie. One day by chance this woman in her fifties happened to come by the bakery. I don't know how she came to tell me the painful story of her son, then fourteen years old, who had become blind as a result of a serious allergy caused by drugs. I was deeply touched by her suffering and the gleam of her blue eyes and her luminous beauty strongly affected me. She was a simple woman, from the countryside around Colmar. I shared my story with her and we became friends. Her calm, compassionate presence made me feel peaceful. Both carrying sadness, we understood each other without even giving the details of our distress.

The other person, Willy Petterschmitt, was one of the leaders of the Mennonite Church of Colmar. (Mennonite: a Protestant movement descended from Anabaptists. Considering infant baptism void because of the absence of any personal act of faith, they rebaptize adults.) At the time, we did not know all the different evangelical churches at all and only knew how to differentiate between the Catholic Church and the Protestant Church. In his work, Willy was called to make visits to share the gospel, and so we were the beneficiaries of his kindness and compassion. He radiated the love of Jesus and regularly spoke to us about the Word of God. The Lord used his servant more than once to calm me down and give me strength to carry on.

As Lucie arrived, sometimes with a huge bouquet of multicolored flowers in her arms or a basket of freshly picked vegetables, Willy the Evangelist came in, smiling and holding the Bible.

Both knew how to be God's envoys to us at times of terrible crisis.

Part Four: The Commitment

Chapter Twenty

Get Up ...

I remember a very special Sunday at the beginning of our return to God. As we respectfully came forward in the church to take the eucharist, I consecrated our relationship to the Lord and asked him to use us in his service. But, suddenly remembering my opposition to religion, I thought my request would be unwelcome, to say the least. Indeed, how could I be so presumptuous today to say I wanted to serve this God whom I had so long despised?

Unaware of my thoughts, Jacques, whose breath I could feel on my neck, bowed to the priest in the white vestment. We both had a visceral desire to touch Heaven where our little boy had preceded us. So, each prayer and each holy communion became a pretext to force open the door.

I had waited a few days before telling Jacques about the conversation, or rather the monologue I had had with the Lord in the cathedral. The statement of my new desires animated him with hope and, grabbing my hand and kissing it gently, his eyes watering with tears, he exclaimed: "Serving God is part of our plans; now we have a goal, Ariane! Please don't cry anymore."

But where? When? And how?

I wanted to leave right away! Anywhere! But to leave, to leave...To flee this throbbing pain that relentlessly tore at my heart without pity.

Jacques, much wiser and calmer than I am, thought that some preparation time was essential. He also wanted to hear the Lord, so he could follow him. Weighed down by my rantings, he hesitated to make a new start when his other half was unable to even stand up. Because I was always overwhelmed by emotional tidal waves dragging me far beyond grief, I was still unfit to start a life elsewhere.

During one of those restless nights of sobbing, a haunting sentence woke me up, tormenting my mind and giving it no rest. I felt it was vitally important not to let it get away, so I grabbed a piece of paper and scribbled in total darkness a series of incoherent words that I did not understand.

Once this surprising gesture was accomplished, I laid my head down on the pillow, satisfied, and fell asleep immediately.

When, the next day, I discovered the sheet with the words so awkwardly scribbled, I read with amazement the injunction that upset the state of fatalistic lethargy into which I had settled: "Get up, and walk!"

This word of authority spoke to me as if God himself were speaking to me. That soft but firm shove in the back, that spiritual push, represented a call from the Lord to move me! That day I felt called upon to take my sadness and walk forward. I finally decided to stand up and follow him.

The story of the paralytic had struck me sometime before. I knew that the miracle performed over 2,000 years ago was also available to me today if I accepted the possibility in faith. *"Which is easier, to say to the paralytic, 'Your sins are forgiven,' or to say: 'Get up, take your mat and walk?'"* (Mark 2:9)

Inspired by the Holy Spirit, I understood that the Lord was healing this poor man not just to be nice and agreeable, but that it was something much bigger and spiritual. This miracle demonstrated God's forgiveness and the new life he offered the paralytic, that he also offered me.

Then, slipping fully into the divine perspective, I saw my suffering as acceptable and the hope of being able to bear it entered the realm of possibility.

I feverishly continued to search the Bible for examples of broken lives like mine which demonstrated how best to respond to the call of Jesus, the Nazarene. I finally found the story of the blind Bartimaeus who addressed Jesus, and cried *"Jesus, Son of David, have mercy on me!"* (Mark

10:47) Despite his infirmity, Bartimaeus ran toward the Master, and having thrown off his cloak, collapsed at his feet.

Identifying with him, I understood in a flash my own situation: like the blind beggar, I had to get up and go. The handicap of my sadness should no longer paralyze me as it had done thus far. I had to cast off my cloak of affliction and stop being obsessed with my pain. Jesus was showing me another path on which I could courageously follow him from now on. The Lord invited me to trust him and to submit to his will so that he could transform my pain into a new way of life, and so that I could finally extinguish my desire to die. I decided then to take my bed and get up for his glory, and maybe also for my own peace.

Faced with my feverish impatience, Jacques, putting his protective arm on my shoulders, calmed me down and assured me of a future in the service of God, in his good time. "Ariane, wait and listen to me; I am sure that the Lord takes our commitment seriously, but it is up to him to take the initiative, because he is the boss. Then in his time we will be informed and blessed because we will be in his plan. In the meantime, we don't move." He then burst out laughing and added: "I'm the little boss, don't forget!" Jacques was right and knew well how to give me hope while calming my ardor. In perfect harmony with him, I trusted Jesus and waited for a sign from him.

One evening at mass, although it certainly did not satisfy my desire to leave, a sentence from the priest quoting Saint Francis de Salle spoke loudly to me: "Blossom where I have planted you. Don't try to run elsewhere..." Jacques was indeed right. This time I accepted a delayed start without grumbling.

Although we had already had a brief experience in a Catholic community, at this point we truly came to understand the importance of the various Christian communities in the region: "The Fellowship of Emmanuel," "The New Path," "The Fellowship of the Lions of Judah" and others. These Christians engaged in announcing the Good News and above all, practiced the gifts of the Spirit mentioned in the Acts of the Apostles. Their simplicity in expressing the proximity of the Kingdom touched us deeply. We longed so much for contact with heaven. It was through these people, guided and imbued by the Holy Spirit, that we received the answers needed to move in the right direction.

Each of us received revelations that were not expressed through visions or voices, but simply through Bible verses that went straight to our hearts. Enlightened by the Spirit, we then understood the hidden meaning of the Biblical sentences and their profound truth, which we exchanged with great joy.

It was God's time, a time when God took his time to teach us, guide us, and protect us. He approached us gently, with the delicacy of a father who opens his arms and his heart to his children, after a painful separation. The Eternal, on tiptoe, as if not to frighten us stooped down and leaned over us, the little creatures that we were. As in the story of the prodigal son in the Bible, there were no reproaches, no sanctions, no admonitions, just an infinite love that still overwhelms me.

"But while he was still a long way off, the father saw him and was filled with compassion for him; he ran to his son, threw his arms around him and kissed him. The father said to the servants, 'Quick! Bring the best robe and put it on him. Put a ring on his finger and sandals on his feet. Bring the fattened calf and kill it. Let's have a feast and celebrate. For this son of mine was dead and is alive again; he was lost and is found.'" (Luke 15: 20, 22-24)

After a year of spiritual quest, we reached our glorious goal, and our search ended. We had found God and had finally become, again, what we had never ceased to be for him--his children.

The reunion was magnificent, on the scale of his love. The Lord of our childhood regained his place of honor and was recognized as the only Master of our adult lives. After all these years of wandering, we came back to the Father and wanted to obey him and follow him, wherever he led us.

It was now up to us to fight to keep what we had gained and to enjoy "God's rest." We understood that walking with Jesus took away neither problems nor suffering. It was only a confident letting go and total obedience to his will that would assure us of serenity. We entered into a dynamic training period nourished by the Holy Spirit, not knowing where this new adventure would lead us. Yet we embarked on it with the passionate audacity of lovers or of those who, having found a treasure, do everything they can to keep it.

Smiling, we identified with the man in the parable who, having found a rare pearl, did everything possible to keep it: *"When he found a pearl of great value, he went away and sold everything he had and bought it."* (Matthew 13:46)

The decision to sell our property was self-evident because the classy BMW coupe and our bakery-croissanterie business weighed very little on the scales of eternity in comparison to our future jobs as servants of the Kingdom. But Jacques felt that, before serving him, we must get to know God better.

Chapter Twenty-One

The Wind is Shifting

T hat is how we came to sell our bakery and go to the International Bible Training Institute for a year of theological studies. This school, located in southern England, welcomed students of all ages from all over the world. This pause in our lives, spent studying the Word and listening to God, marked us for life with lessons that accompanied us along our path.

Rid of all forms of religiosity, we felt free to welcome what the Spirit wanted to give us, and we made the serious decision to become disciples of Christ, whatever the cost and whatever happened. That is what we wanted to be, and what by his Grace we would become.

Our return to France after this long spiritual bath was difficult in every way.

Still living emotionally on a little cloud, we found the landing rough and I felt like we were making "ground refusals" which was not brilliant for our reputation as skilled skydivers! From mixing with the angels, chatting with the Lord, curling up against the Father's chest and enjoying his hugs, we found normal life harsh and monotonous.

Trusting in divine providence, but still a little worried all the same, we thought it imperative to find a job. A few days later an English teaching position became available, and I replaced the departing teacher on short notice. For his part, Jacques found a job selling wooden houses and verandas. So while I was giving my lessons in Colmar, he crisscrossed Alsace, Lorraine. and the Vosges.

We had returned to the big house in Ingersheim, where my mother happily agreed that we could convert part of it. After the renovation, it would become a charming duplex. Several years after the start of that work, in March 1998, after several strokes, death took my mother away from us for eternity.

We had kept our son's ashes until then, but when my mother died, we thought that Frantz should join his grandmother in the grave; she had loved him so much and he had loved her in return with all his ten-year-old little boy's heart. I was extremely sad when she left, but the comfort of believing that she had joined her grandson in the light was sweet and reassuring to me. I experienced her absence as a new wound, but this time I knew that it would heal. It was not the heartbreak caused by the death of Frantz, but the grief of having lost sight of a mother whom I admired, whom I loved, and who had brought me such tenderness and compassion at the most excruciating point of my life. I think of her often and look forward to seeing her again when we are all together in paradise.

***

At that time, our lives seemed to achieve relative normalcy and the project of settling down more comfortably gave us a new impulse. Still, we weren't completely satisfied! We liked our two jobs which gave us sufficient financial comfort to foresee a stable future. But the desire to serve God concretely grew more pressing every day. We unabashedly and joyfully talked about our spiritual discovery. With his overflowing enthusiasm and passionate character, Jacques "cut off many ears," like Peter, the fiery disciple, defending Jesus during his arrest in the Garden of Gethsemane.

Sometimes, I admit, we lacked tact, but can there be compatibility between passion and delicacy?

Our way of life, conventional and comfortable, seemed tasteless to us, without the salt of which Jesus speaks in the Gospel. We were frustrated.

"Okay, we want to follow Jesus and serve him, but nothing's on the horizon in Alsace and then we wanted to go to Australia nine years ago, remember? Well now there's no stopping us, let's go!"

Then with a mischievous wink, Jacques added, "We're going to complicate the Lord's plans a bit, but maybe He has a job for us there—what do you think?"

I understood what it meant to "complicate the plans of the Lord," because generally it was understood that serving the Lord was to be accomplished within the Church or in related associations. Sometime before, while we were trying to find our way, the need for the absolute submission to the love of God had prompted us to consider retreating to a monastery. But on the other hand, going back to creating a business abroad proved to be a challenge and a kind of provocation to the Lord, because there was really nothing spiritual about it.

Understanding our parent-child relationship with our Eternal Father gave us the opportunity to practice this freedom of speech and action. We were about to change course and, as Jacques said with confidence and great respect, the Lord would be with us in Australia!

Restlessness had overcome us! I fully agreed with my alter ego: we would go.

"Why not?" I replied with a mischievous smile.

I wanted to follow him, my Jacques. I would let him rule our lives and try a new adventure. I knew that he would do nothing without God's agreement and that only God could suspend or encourage our new project.

We discussed this seriously and started making plans. The legendary optimism that characterized us led us to think that we were still young enough, or rather not yet too old to take the risk. "Still, it's borderline, especially for you!" Jacques joked since I was a year older!

Sweeping away all the obstacles, our decision was made. This time we were going to achieve what we had failed to do in America. The immigration papers were requested immediately at the Australian Embassy in Paris. We sent the necessary documents off in the mail, and feeling light,

I left to lead an English conversation class, my head filled with visions of kangaroos!

When I got home late that afternoon, funny news awaited me. Apparently, the Lord had heard us, and he disagreed with our plan! "Ariane, sit down. Josiane called. We wanted to go to Australia, didn't we? I believe the Lord doesn't want that! How about Albania?"

Albania!? I knew absolutely nothing about that country! I was stunned by the dramatic change. It was Jacques' turn to conspire with the Lord as I had done a few months before!

Josiane, the founder of MEDAIR, had called that afternoon, explaining that the organization needed us in El Basan. Sensing that God wanted us in the Balkans, Jacques had almost agreed but was waiting for me to confirm his answer. The war in Kosovo was raging and the NGO (non-governmental organization) had been commissioned by the Swiss government to financially support Kosovar refugees as well as Albanian families.

The Lord was thwarting our plans and not letting us start a business in Australia. We did not yet understand the reason, but we trusted him, feeling perfectly at peace to begin this new chapter. So, on June 14, 1999, we flew to Tirana. What a wonderful gift to feel like a messenger from Jesus on my birthday! This first mission would be followed by many others since we never again ceased to be at the service of the poorest, in the name of the Lord.

Was this the last piece of the waiting game of our lives? And had we finally found our place in the Kingdom of God?

In any case, this work perfectly complimented our burning desire to bring the love of Jesus, in a concrete way, by modestly becoming his arms, his hands, and his heart on earth. We would become his co-workers, wherever he would send us.

We embarked on this humanitarian project as quickly as possible because we felt a sharp tension between the locals and the newly arrived refugees. Financial aid would no doubt soften the aggressiveness of the Albanians, as the massive arrival of hundreds of thousands of refugees to their country made them nervous and ready to fight. The Kosovars, for their part, having the possibility of buying their food, became less indebted to their hosts, thus regaining some of their dignity. This program of "Cash for Shelter" made it possible to relieve the tension between the two enemy brothers and to nip an internal conflict in the bud.

When the peace treaty was signed, the refugees immediately returned to Kosovo, but the fighting had greatly damaged Albania. So we stayed in El Basan for a few more months to help repair the station and renovate the area. At that point, we learned of the rampant corruption and trafficking that was poisoning this country. Albania, in the hands of prominent organized crime bosses and wavering honest politicians, would be hard-pressed to recover.

When we returned from this mission, the MEDAIR NGO offered us two options to continue working for them: Africa or Afghanistan.

Having spent over twelve years of his life on oil rigs in Muslim countries, Jacques was not very enthusiastic about the idea of going to Kabul. He remembered how challenging it had been to lead his teams, especially during the time of Ramadan. So, settling in a country where the Taliban dictatorship was in control and where Sharia law was applied to the letter had zero appeal for him.

On the other hand, this country had intrigued me since I was young. I had read *Les Cavaliers* by Joseph Kessel when I was eighteen and the images described by that remarkable writer had so thrilled me that I had dreamed of seeing for myself what was hidden behind his words. Like the disciple Thomas of the Gospel, I have always struggled to believe without seeing!

So could my wish come true?

Chapter Twenty-Two

The Afghan Land

February 3, 2000, we found ourselves in Kabul.

We arrived in a splendid land, although one marred by the blood of decades of war. The invasion of the Russians and the long years of bitter fighting to drive them out resulted in massive numbers of civilian deaths. Then the civil war, for which Kabul was the theater, destroyed one-quarter of the Afghan capital. The belligerents, famous warlords vying for power, regularly fired rockets and other explosives from one hill to another. Buildings then collapsed on inhabitants who did not have time to go out onto the street or hide in their cellars. During fierce battles, the panicked population, often in the direct path of the shells, did not have much chance of escaping. In each Kabul family, several dead are still mourned from that period.

The massacres against certain ethnic groups, revenge killings, rapes, and all the cruel abuses left the Afghan people with perpetual trauma. Indeed, the warlords, even more than the foreign armies, set their own capital on fire.

In 1996, the rise to power of the Taliban (plural of Talib--the Taliban are students of Islamic theology and of Pashtun origin) plunged the city into total darkness. Everything had frozen and life had stopped. So much ugliness, filth, misery, and injustice evoked a nightmare continuing day after day, with no hope of awakening.

At that time, Kabul, a traumatized, disfigured, and moribund city, survived only through international aid. No electricity, no restaurants, no women in the streets, no schools, no games, no laughter, no music, no kites… Everything was forbidden; no fun allowed.

Barbarians governed the country. These fanatics with kohl-smeared eyes and hateful looks practiced unfair justice and applied Sharia laws to the letter with sadistic glee. I immediately hated them, those who forbade any education for girls, who stoned women and tracked down men with whips to push them into mosques at prayer time. And I hated their behavior when I saw poor unfortunates hanged for some foolish or unjust reason, and young boys forced against their wills to attend madrasas (Koranic schools), where they were brainwashed and later used as living bombs.

Islamist indoctrination made them believe they would go to heaven if they killed unbelievers, Christians, or Jews. The hatred distilled month after month into the hearts of these young people was also directed against the Hazaras, an ethnic group abhorred by the Taliban. Because of the Hazaras' Shiite faith (the branch of Islam claiming to be followers of Ali, the son-in-law of the prophet), they had become heretics in the Taliban's eyes. Setting themselves up as the guardians of religion, these intolerant Sunnis (the branch of Islam representing the majority of Afghans) bestowed on themselves the right, in the name of God, to eradicate the Hazara population which supposedly polluted the purity of their Islamic nation.

How to accept so much injustice and not immediately rebel against this fanatical madness? My mind, my heart, my whole being revolted.

Bearded men were everywhere in the streets, wielding clubs, whips, and Kalashnikovs, and spewing Koranic verses. Terrorizing the population, they also frightened me, because we never knew where their fury would land. A simple exchange of words could end in a pool of blood. I saw them whip children and slash men, and I'll never forget their hideous grins and their hatred for those who didn't think like them.

Jacques and I became aware of the extreme misery of the Afghans at that time. From France, we had not been able to properly assess the distress of a country controlled by religious radicals, claiming to be the only guarantors of the precepts of Islam. They lived jihad with all the horror of so-called holy wars, but which I think are only a reflection of hell, under the inspiration of Satan.

Devastated and deeply saddened, we could not remain impassive before the annihilation of the Hazara community. Our rebellious natures and sense of justice compelled us to act in a more personal way, and our faith in Jesus called us to action. Bringing his love, especially to these who had been banished from the land by this inept government, turned out to be the least we could do. It became our goal, even if it meant taking risks.

But…how?

After our eight-month mission with the Swiss organization, we were hired by the director of a huge United Nations project that focussed on supporting more than 5,000 beneficiaries chosen from the poorest populations of Kabul.

The Afghans were all extremely poor since no work was available and the economy was stagnating at an all-time low. Women, who were particularly vulnerable, were prohibited from leaving their homes without covering themselves with a burka (a covering that hides the body from head to toe). In their rare escapes, these blue ghosts had to be accompanied by a mahram (a male member of the family escort, from a teenager to an old man). Sometimes one saw on a deserted street a few such figures with a boy of eight or ten years old, who was supposed to protect their virtue!

Through this new job, I got out of the office quite often as a women's program manager, creating and running pasta-making workshops all over town. I traveled regularly around Kabul to oversee the manufacture of spaghetti and monitor its distribution. The products, intended for widows and the poorest, would be given to them if no corruption diverted it to others.

At the end of the month, I carried, well hidden under my veils, the salaries of the women in charge of the workshops; the others were paid in rice. The masters of Kabul had only authorized us to pay in kilos of rice and certainly not in cash. So once again I twisted the law with a pleasure rarely equaled. I was taking a big risk carrying this money, but the satisfaction of breaking the unjust law and the delight of cheating them was well worth all the risk! I wanted so much to help the Afghan women, whose salaries provided for the basic needs of their families, that I didn't care about the danger.

One time, entering the workshop, I lifted my veils and showed them my special belt stuffed with dollars. My friends giggled and asked me how many roadblocks I had crossed, thus calculating the number of enemies fooled! Later, sipping a hot tea, they laughed out loud at my tricks, and I enjoyed their newfound smiles.

These brief moments of hilarity were unfortunately overshadowed when we were made aware of the contents of the bags of rice that we were distributing to them. Indeed, the tons of rice donated by the United Nations and purchased in Pakistan were filled with dirt. I was ashamed and outraged when the women showed me what they had found in their bundles. At least three kilos of the twenty-five allocated were made up of stones, cigarette butts, and wisps of straw. We knew about the enmity between Afghanistan and Pakistan, but we would never have imagined the lack of consideration and the total lack of compassion of the Pakistanis towards their Afghan neighbors.

After several unanswered complaints, we decided one day to meet with the food aid manager. Unable to bear it any longer, Jacques angrily threw open a bag of rice full of cigarette butts and gravel, asking him if he would dare to give this food of filthy quality to people suffering from malnutrition. I was stunned to hear the service director respond with a wry sigh that it was not his fault, and that, in any case when you are hungry, it is better than nothing!

We left disgusted, and we concluded that there was "something rotten" in the kingdom of the humanitarians.

We had already struggled so hard to start this project and now we had to fight for food support worthy of the name! I felt unworthy of my status as an expatriate, faced with these poor, destitute, and unfairly treated women. I was angry with the United Nations, which on the whole seemed to care more about its reputation than the people. The statistics quoted staggering numbers of tons of food donated, but officials did not bother to find out how it was distributed or what its quality was. The reports we read were smooth and clean, like the cars and offices of the people who worked there. So we wondered: how were they really helping?

Why did the management turn a blind eye to the corruption of its local employees, some of whom supplemented their income by selling in the bazaar what they should have distributed to the poor? We were stunned by the negligence and flippancy of the people in charge of the programs. Moreover, Jacques, as the head of mission, had had a hard time convincing the Taliban that this aid would also necessarily involve Afghan women.

The Taliban leader, Mullah Omar, had issued a new law excluding women from all work. So Jacques had used subtle strategies to try to influence the local leaders of Kabul, without whose agreement we could not start the project. It had taken him three months, three long months, waiting for permission from those callous self-styled princes! Three endless months while the most vulnerable people were dying of hunger, fatigue, and despair.

Sometimes, Jacques asked me to accompany him to the offices to demonstrate that the work of women would in no way be controlled by a man since his wife would be responsible for it. Lowering my head under my veils, I assumed a modest air and avoided meeting their gaze since the Taliban forbade women to look men in the eye. Dressed as an Afghan, I measured the difficulty of being a woman in this country—wearing socks on my feet when it was 104 degrees in the shade so as not to expose my ankles to the men, I was also covered by long fabrics in bland colors, disguising my female body which was seen as a source of shame.

In this religious culture, the woman absolutely did not represent the indispensable help that the God of the Bible gave to man, but rather his scapegoat. The Quran states that people of the weaker sex are only half as valuable as men, so all abuse is permitted. In Afghanistan, the uneducated population considers the woman as an object to make little Muslims and do the housework. She has no rights, except to obey and be silent.

At the end of the three months we had waited to obtain the authorizations necessary to begin the project, Jacques, at the end of his patience, dropped all formal politeness. "This project will never start for lack of agreement with the government," he told the Taliban one morning, bewildered that a foreigner was speaking to them with authority. "The money will go to Africa where the needs are also critical. Too bad for Afghanistan and for you who, in the eyes of the world, will be seen as men indifferent to the misfortune of their own people. You will have a terrible reputation with the international community, which already criticizes you harshly…" he added with an annoyed expression, praying to God that his threat would shake them up.

Facetious and exasperated at the same time, he had been tempted to tell them that the money would go to Israel, the sworn enemy of Muslims, but had fortunately held back at the last moment. With Afghan prisons not offering very comfortable hospitality, and the Taliban having no sense of humor, I think that was a good thing!

Three days after that meeting, the protocol was signed and the program finally launched. Engineers hired for road repairs and other construction work warmly thanked Jacques for his determination and diplomacy. The signing of this agreement gave three thousand employees work essential to their families' survival. Happy for them, we could easily imagine them sharing the good news when they got home.

For my part, I supervised the women's project and the proper use of ingredients. Forty-one workshops were created throughout all districts of Kabul--all the districts, except where the Hazaras lived in fear and without any help. When, by chance, I met a woman of this ethnicity and wanted her to join the program, it caused a major stir because, for the rest of the Afghans, the Hazaras had to remain isolated and confined to their ghetto: "They are dirty, cruel, violent and illiterate!" affirmed my Tajik and Pashtun (the two largest ethnic groups in Afghanistan) colleagues.

This minority suffered from despicable discrimination that previous governments had encouraged and that the Taliban continued to exercise with incredible violence. In Kabul, rumors circulated about the massacres of this population, mainly in the villages of Hazarajat, where a scorched earth policy was used against the despised ethnic group. Those who managed to escape the carnage told us of the movements of families at night, the hasty escapes into the mountains around Bamiyan, and the hiding places in the caves near the large 1400-year-old Buddhas, the same Buddhas that the Taliban would indiscriminately blow up a few months later.

We wondered how we could help them. This program included more than 5,000 people, including about 1,500 women. In the difficult discussions that Jacques had had with the Taliban, they had imposed a limit of no more than twenty-one women allowed to gather together in the workshops at a time. The Taliban feared gatherings of women, which could inspire rebellions or incite harmful thoughts. This forced us to double the workshops but also to hire more instructors, which increased the number of families supported.

It was clear that their fear of women was one of the causes of their relentless desire to enslave them. They drove out the intellectuals and stifled any attempt at rebellion. Having experienced that changes of attitude often come through women, these men, most of whom were illiterate, sought to permanently muzzle Afghan women and prohibit them from any form of education.

However, I knew some who did not accept being under the yoke of illiterate tyrants and who, despite threats of being beaten in public places or stoned, continued intellectual pursuits and defiantly educated their own children.

Among them was Mariam, a young female judge, who was recruited along with her friends, Fatima and Soheila, to help me run the pasta centers. This female trio became for me synonymous with hope in such a dismal environment. With cunning, we fought together the ridiculous rules of life imposed on Afghan women and found all sorts of tricks to circumvent obstacles and protect women. Our complicity was boundless and we delighted in the tricks we would play on the bearded men to whom I brazenly lied, assuring them that the women never took off their burkas. We also placed a prayer rug prominently, to show how much God was honored and prayed to in the middle of making the spaghetti. No woman ever knelt in the middle of this grotesque staging!

Then one day, the leader of the Taliban expressed a desire to visit our project. The program devoted to men did not interest him. In vain Jacques boasted about the repair of the karez (systems bringing water through underground channels) and the construction of sewers which the men worked on, but nothing seemed to move him. He was singularly focused on the work of the women.

The next morning, seven fellows in turbans arrived at the office and abruptly announced that we had to go to the site right away. Jacques, his eyebrows arched, gave me a quick glance and I immediately understood the difficulty: how were we going to fit them in a five-seater car when there were nine of us?

The situation became comical when they strictly applied their sexist segregation that prevented them from sitting next to me. I saw them pile into the back seat and into the trunk. Hardly repressing a giggle, I saw how they punished themselves with their intolerance as I comfortably settled in next to the driver.

My presence could not be dispensed with, as no man could enter the workshop except the Supreme Leader of the Taliban, who was also in charge of the Vice and Virtue department. So I would accompany him on the tour while Jacques waited with the men outside.

In the middle of August, it was a scorching 113 degrees outside, and driving across the city in a cramped car with no air conditioning was challenging, to say the least. On arrival, crimson faces, turbans askew, kohl around their eyes mixed with sweat dripping into their beards, the suffocating Taliban had lost their luster. I still see them take a few unsteady steps to stretch their legs, then roll up their turbans, belch spit and dust, and finally walk away from the car, forgetting their three comrades stuck in the trunk.

I took pleasure in forgetting all about them too, even though I heard them thumping and yelling to be let out! I admit, just knowing they were packed together in that trunk as hot as a furnace gave me immense pleasure! My Afghan friends and colleagues imprisoned in their blue veils were waiting for us on the sidewalk. Without a word, our thoughts met: the Taliban locked in the trunk were in turn suffering for a few minutes from the suffocation they imposed on women under their burkas!

Eighteen years after that incident, I still remember it clearly, as grotesque as it was hilarious, and the giggles barely muffled by the blue mesh of the burkas still resonate. It was only a joke, but we savored every second of it. And then, as all good things must come to an end, a Taleb came to free our prisoners, who, regaining their composure and their sticks, resumed their dirty work. Everything returned to normal in the land of mistreatment and iniquity. I interpreted this as a wink from God, humorously encouraging me to support my Afghan friends.

Chapter Twenty-Three

Burkas

W e were always closely watched by the authorities in Kabul since we worked with women. The head of the office of Vice and Virtue assigned one of their own to scrutinize us in all our actions. This Talib in charge of controlling us was the father of one of the wives of Mullah Omar, the infamous leader of the Taliban movement. After a few months of observations on both sides, Jacques and he became friendly.

One day, at the end of the morning, returning from a workshop with him, I heard Jacques invite him to share our meal. As soon as I walked through the door I threw off my veil as usual and asked my host if it embarrassed him. With a smile that conveyed all the irony in the world, he assured me that he didn't care at all. Then, pulling Jacques aside, he undid his shirt and showed him his many scars. In interrupted sentences of long sighs and wry looks, our spy/controller revealed his allergy to obeying stupid orders and his aversion to continuing to fight for an ideology in which he no longer believed. He also made no secret of his desire to flee Afghanistan and asked if we could help him obtain a visa for France or Germany. It was the first time we had come across a demoralized "theology student," devoid of arrogance and without hubris. Handing him the medicine he had asked for, I noticed his crestfallen face and the sadness in his eyes. A feeling of pity came over me.

A few years later, after the fall of the Taliban, Jacques met him by chance in a government ministry and was surprised at his appearance: he had changed his headgear and swapped his turban for the cap of Commander Massoud, the sworn enemy of the Taliban! In Afghanistan, political alliances followed by betrayals and abrupt denials are frequent. The enemy then becomes the friend, and the opportunistic ally turns into a fierce adversary. Nothing is ever gained and reversals of such situations are common.

His failed departure for Europe and the disappointment of having served a regime, first out of conviction and then because of the impossibility of leaving it, had made him bitter. Like many others, this ordinary man, certainly not fond of war, was sucked into the senseless turmoil of Afghan history, of which the reign of the Taliban marked one of its darkest passages.

When Jacques told me about this chance meeting, happy to hear news of him, I remembered the man in the white turban, with the jade-colored eyes bordered by disproportionately long and silky lashes. He had the somewhat mysterious beauty of the princes of the Persian Empire from which his ancestors probably descended. Yet it was not his physical features and gentle gaze that had charmed me, but rather how he had done his job as a spy. I had always sensed a certain timidity and great restraint in his questioning, and I had the impression that he was seeking to protect us.

While I was thinking of him, memories of that tumultuous time came flooding back, and his benevolence still touches me to this day. Indeed his sound advice saved us from serious trouble, especially during an inspection by the highest Taliban authority whose visit was planned. This envoy of Mullah Omar represented an absolute danger. Responsible for judging and inflexibly applying Sharia law throughout Afghanistan, he scared us. I prayed for inspiration at the right time and for a foolproof strategy, because the outcome of his visit would be crucial for the continuation of the project.

Sometime earlier, the Vice and Virtue religious police had contacted us to evaluate how we were enforcing the ban on meetings between two people of the opposite sex. These gentlemen prided themselves on guaranteeing the virtue of Afghan women and ensuring that their rules were strictly followed.

The night before the visit, Jacques and I couldn't sleep, and I worried until dawn, trying to think of the best way to avoid angering this man who had already brutally cracked down on an emergency hospital run by an Italian NGO. His henchmen had entered by force, killing two guards in the process, then finding male doctors having lunch with female staff, had thrown the sick and seriously injured patients out on the sidewalk. Smashed serum bottles, trampled medicines, screams, and beatings had ended their violent raid. This clinic took care of everyone without distinction. Mutilated and wounded fighters from opposing sides returning from the front found themselves in hospital beds side by side. Whether they were Taliban or Massoud soldiers, the ethos of the NGO was to treat any injured person. That day the Taliban, in their blind fury, did not even realize the gross mistake of having ejected their own soldiers from the hospital and putting them in mortal danger! The event had been reported to us shortly before the terrifying announcement of the infamous visit. This left us very concerned, especially me since I would be on the front line with the women under their burkas during the visit.

As I was thinking about it methodically and analyzing the situation. I developed a plan! With all my strength I wanted to defend my Afghan girls and not interrupt the project which not only helped them financially but gave them the opportunities to get together and rekindle a social life that had been cut off when the buffoons had come to power. These meetings did them good because the workshops nurtured a chain of solidarity and sharing, essential for solving everyday problems. Their practical intelligence developed unexpected survival mechanisms to handle the most preposterous challenges. I liked to listen to their conversations expressing their hope for a world free of the obstacles to living normally. Above all, I enjoyed hearing their laughter because that reconnected them to life, but also because they led me to join them in this desire for self-transcendence and courage. So, I realized that even as I was helping them a little, they were helping me enormously.

It was therefore necessary to organize and select at least two workshops where no man or even a teenage boy could possibly encounter these ladies.

If I could prove the physical impossibility of a mixed meeting, I might have won part of the battle.

Mariam and I located the ideal center which, after a few modifications, would present the least danger. Sly, I had also spotted another workshop to visit in case the first location was refused. In this country it is always good to have a plan B and C; sometimes even the whole alphabet is necessary!

We almost had everything planned...

That morning, as I was waiting at the center, I received a signal from Jacques warning me of the imminent arrival of the car in which he was riding, surrounded by the scrutinizer and our spy. Describing the event eighteen years later, I still feel my heart racing and my throat tightening. Such deep terror is not easily forgotten.

The man in black entered and with a piercing gaze appraised me, judged me, and condemned me simply for my status as a Western woman. The Afghan women were shaking under their burkas, and I had a hard time not doing the same. Despite everything, I tried to answer his questions as naturally as possible and to keep my voice steady. Hypocritically, we had hung verses from the Koran on the wall, and a prayer rug pointing toward Mecca greeted visitors. Outside, a scaffolded wall with old containers and boxes separated the yard so that our driver delivering the flour couldn't even see the blue shadows. In the entrance hall, a thick curtain hid the staircase leading to the floor where a recluse lived, a fourteen-year-old orphan, the only survivor of a family massacred by the friends of this religious leader.

We thought we had eliminated all risk when suddenly the unthinkable arose. As I was explaining the course of the workshop's activities, the Taleb-spy-friend discreetly, but with a distraught look, pointed out to me the dangerous object: an empty Coca-Cola bottle lying innocently in a corner of the room! It was absolutely necessary to prevent the religious despot from seeing it and allowing his pitiless wrath fall on the poor sinners that we represented.

I coughed to alert Mariam hidden under her burka, and whose shoes I had recognized, but neither my cryptic language nor my frantic signs penetrated the blue mesh covering her eyes. So using a subtle diversionary tactic, I jabbered a few sentences in Dari (the second official language spoken in Afghanistan after Pashto) about the difficulty of finding the spaghetti-cutting machines. And, as I dragged the bearded colossus towards the dented equipment, I took advantage of his turned gaze to boldly kick the evidence of sin behind the sacks of flour. Phew, that was close!

As the Taliban did not support any contact with "the great Satan" embodied by America, he would undoubtedly have closed the project, since by drinking the drink originating in the USA, the Afghan women would certainly have been tempted by other poisons such as music, dancing, and laughter. The authorization that Jacques had really won would have been useless to guarantee the legitimacy of the contract since Sharia prevails over any other form of legislation.

A few days later, congratulated by the ladies for having made the illicit bottle disappear, I drank large swigs of Coca-Cola with them, toasting the health of the spy/taleb/savior, and we laughed at the clumsiness of the hoodwinked scoundrel. Sometimes, I told myself, it's fun to live dangerously! Nietzsche, the German philosopher, might have been right.

Chapter Twenty-Four

September

On September 10, 2001, after midnight, a series of violent explosions jolted us awake, and we jumped out of bed to see what was going on! It appeared the airport was busy. Scanning the sky streaked with all the colors of the rainbow, we stared dumbfounded at a squad of planes and helicopters. The last rampart against the Taliban had fallen the day before under the bullets of two fake journalists who had come to interview Ahmad Shah Massoud, the hero of the war against the Russians. This shrewd strategist and brave soldier died as a result of the well-laid-out plan. On September 9th, after several failures, the Taliban's evil design finally succeeded. Mortally shot in the face when the camera of one of the terrorists exploded, Commander Massoud succumbed to his injuries in the helicopter transporting him to the Takhar hospital. We learned later that the air raid we were witnessing was avenging the death of the famous Tajik. That night, the Taliban ammunition arsenal stored in a hangar at the airport exploded in its entirety, creating an unexpected fireworks display.

The radiant sky of unreal colors was not to celebrate Jacques' birthday as I had initially suggested to him, but an event that opened the way to tragedy.

The assassination of the man whom the Afghans and the international press called "the Lion of Panshir" really represented an alarm for the whole world and for Afghanistan in particular, because this tragedy demonstrated a resounding victory for Al Qaeda whose leader, Osama bin Laden, had ordered the killing.

We had heard about him from the mullahs in Kabul who arrogantly explained to us that Afghanistan would no longer need money from the West and that unbelievers could pack their bags. They now had a savior in the person of Osama, a close friend of Mullah Omar, who would provide the country with his protection and a windfall of money.

Afghanistan, finally rid of the infidels, would reveal the original purity of Islam. Then the world would recognize the prophet Mohammad to be the only one capable of showing the way to God. Some religious Afghans who had become our friends warned us that foreigners would have to leave.

Then everything accelerated. Our instincts were on high alert since the attack on Massoud, and we felt imminent danger and a relentless advance towards dark horizons. Some aid workers from a German humanitarian organization were denounced and then arrested for proselytizing. Now they had been languishing in a sordid Kabul prison for several days. We knew them well since they had lived next door, and we had gone over to pray with them every Friday. On the evening of the tragedy, as we were returning from the office, our panic-stricken guard signaled us to be quiet. Despite having been brutally interrogated by the Taliban just before our arrival, he gave them no compromising information about us; his friendship saved us.

About a dozen men invaded the house of the disgraced NGO next door to us. They engaged in a meticulous search, knocking over and smashing everything in their path. Terrified by hearing the commotion all night, my fear turned to panic when I learned in the early morning that they were high on hashish, which multiplied their violence all the more. Samshed, our kind guard, feared as much for us as for himself, because if we were guilty of being Christians, he was also guilty of studying medicine, since all education had been prohibited.

I trembled at the sight of the few forbidden women's magazines and no longer able to bear the bawling of our new neighbors, I threw the forbidden readings and my Bible into the chimney fire that Jacques had just lit at my request. Not proud of my gesture, but unable to manage a paralyzing fear that sapped all my courage, I watched sadly as the flames licked up the pages of God's Word. Jacques, calm and valiant, saved his Bible and advised me with humor to learn it by heart for the next time!

We still had no news of our friends in prison and the Red Cross negotiated few visits. The city seemed frozen, its already heavy atmosphere becoming suffocating.

Returning to a restless, but restorative sleep at the headquarters of the Medair organization, we regained some strength after many sleepless nights. The news grew more alarming with each passing day, revealing an explosive and uncontrollable situation.

We attended a rushed security meeting, and what we heard terrified us. The Taliban, having tolerated our presence on Afghan soil so far, were becoming increasingly nervous and aggressive toward foreigners. The tension rose a notch when we heard the head of security reading us their new rules. It stipulated a dozen commandments that would be implemented immediately and were to be signed by each expatriate.

One of the articles stated that foreign women would now wear a yellow burka to differentiate them from Afghan women and thus be spotted more easily!

Then came a whole series of orders not to be transgressed, on pain of suffering the same punishments as the Afghans in the Kabul stadium, where the hands of thieves were cut off, adulterers lynched and petty criminals simply whipped. Glancing at us knowingly, we all smiled at the mention of the ban on eating haram (religiously prohibited) food since our suitcases were filled with forbidden charcuterie on our return from France. Would we really risk being beaten for a slice of ham? Or even for listening to prohibited Western music?

The great frustration of no longer being able to go to the United Nations guest house undoubtedly elicited the heaviest sigh. We had enjoyed meeting new people and drinking an occasional beer there, even if Jacques found it a little lukewarm for his taste!

The next day, we learned from one of our engineers about the tragedy of the World Trade Center towers, because without electricity or television, we had no access to news media. We couldn't believe what Yasin was explaining, and his weak English did not guarantee a good translation of the information from Voice of America. Moreover, the Afghans have the curious habit of relating bad news with smiling faces, so we thought it might be some kind of joke, in very bad taste.

The horror of the event would exceed all comprehension.

Ten minutes later, all summoned to the conference room, a reliable source confirmed the unbelievable truth, and we had to leave the office immediately to pack our bags.

With tears in my eyes, despite my anguish, I refused to leave right away. How could we leave this country? How could we abandon this vulnerable population that relied on us? How would we be able to forget this feeling of shame and the nagging guilt that I felt welling up inside me? And yet that's what we did, but only after gathering the sensitive papers that put our Afghan employees at risk. Living in a waking nightmare, I watched in shock as the shredder gobbled up and demolished my friends' pay slips.

We were evacuated on September 13th aboard the last plane to leave Kabul. Flying over the Hindu Kush range towards Pakistan, I couldn't hold back my tears. Everyone seemed relieved and calm. My gaze was lost in the clouds as I questioned the heavens about my broken dream: to take care of the poor children of Kabul one day. I thought that I would never come back to this country again and that our project had collapsed along with the Twin Towers.

Chapter Twenty-Five

Escape

The small plane gently touched down on the tarmac of Islamabad airport and taxied to a stop between two large Pakistan International Airlines planes. The passengers, whose faces reflected relief and concern at the same time, started to disembark.

Our life in Kabul, so disconnected from the rest of the world, had not allowed us to really understand the situation and we had still not faced the tragic horror of the World Trade Center. Moreover, having seen no image of the magnitude of the drama, we did not know exactly what had happened and the true extent of the event. Had it been a small plane flying over Manhattan that accidentally hit a tower? Was there a lot of damage? Was it catastrophic? What might explain the sudden order given to flee Afghanistan?

For my part, this run-for-your-life exodus left me with the bitter taste of regrets and broken promises.

I was thinking more and more of my friends, Fatima, with whom I had conversed the day before my departure, and Mariam, my kind accomplice, who gave me a letter and lapis-lazuli jewelry to show her friendship. And then what would become of Soheila and her old husband? Married at fourteen, she became this sick old man's insurance and his surest support. A love relationship had finally developed in this forced marriage and the story of this united couple had touched me. How would her family survive without her salary?

In my mind, I had also made a promise to the poor children of Kabul. My heart twisted with sadness at the thought of little Magid, whose pleading gaze melted our hearts. We had seen too many of these children digging through heaps of garbage, feverishly searching for the remains of well-filled plates from satiated expatriates. I felt so helpless in front of their grimy faces and simple requests. They asked for food, pencils, and notebooks, but also games. The few little girls in the street had asked me for dolls. How could I help them all? How could I give them something better than dollars? How could we create something for them, and only for them? Having been treated so unfairly by life, we had finally come up with a plan for them. But what would it be now?

Under the barbarism of the Taliban regime, children were the only ones to bring money home when the father was absent, dead, or taken away by religious militias. Mothers, banned from work and confined indoors, had no choice but to send their children out to the very dangerous streets to try and find work.

All sorts of odd jobs presented themselves: scrounging up fallen fruits and vegetables at the bazaar, collecting plastic bottles and bits of metal and wood to sell, polishing the shoes of expatriates, begging, and burning herbs to chase away evil spirits. These kids with sad, sunken eyes approached big, comfortable cars in the street, then they put their skinny little arms inside and waved tin cans filled with smoking herbs around. We coughed for long minutes after their incursion and easily understood that the spirits sickened by this unbreathable air quickly fled! Filthy, nimble hands then grabbed on the fly the few afghanis and sweets that I always put in my bag in anticipation of these encounters.

Our own project was born thanks to these street urchins. It was inspired by their painful situation, yes, but also by so much more. Their charming faces, their heartfelt playfulness, and the way they surprised us with their disarming smiles also motivated us. At the height of their distress, they defended the life that was in them, their life made of will, courage, and endurance. Left to their own devices, they developed remarkable survival skills. By just meeting them and observing them, I began to admire them. Yes, they commanded respect, these clever and hardworking little kids, these strong children determined to get by and support their mothers and siblings.

Without them knowing it, Jacques and I had promised them that we would do everything we could to help them live and prepare for their future. Out of their need to be fed, educated, and to have the chance to play as all children deserve, the initial plans for the project were drawn up, for the organization that we would one day create.

The memory of my son, immensely present in my life, no doubt also pushed me to act beyond what was purely rational. Not taking into account the obstacles or the dangers, I instinctively felt that my own survival depended on these little gray ghosts of the Afghan capital.

As a United Nations car drove us back from the airport, I played back these images of the gloomy streets where children waited for the slightest opportunity to get help. I sadly noticed the enormous difference between the two capitals during this half-hour journey, where the joyful cries of the children contrasted so strongly with my little Kabulis. Islamabad, a city swarming with passers-by in colorful clothes, looked like a place bursting with life, while we had experienced a constant sense of death in the Afghan capital.

We finally arrived at the offices of the humanitarian organization. And there, we began to understand, with the greatest dismay, the true dimensions of the horrifyingly surreal attacks in New York. The spectacle of the towers collapsing like sandcastles seemed dreamlike to us and the direct descent into this nightmare astounded us. We thought with compassion of our American friends, but also of the rest of the world, which, like us, would never be the same again.

It was high time to buy a plane ticket: airline companies serving Pakistan were withdrawing one after another, and no one knew what was going to happen in this part of the world. The temperature of the Pakistani summer rose to the maximum, literally and figuratively, because soon no planes would be allowed to take off. Expatriates panicked at the thought of the possibility of having to stay there in the event of war or bombing.

Finally, after some negotiating with travel agencies, we got two plane tickets for flights the next day to the airport closest to Alsace: Frankfurt. Relieved to depart this increasingly tense country, we began to gather our things.

Our colleagues in Islamabad were worried about our fate. Without any news from us after the attacks, they thought that we had missed the last plane leaving Afghanistan. The surprise of seeing us on their doorstep provoked a cascade of laughter and affectionate embraces, as we were invited to stay for dinner.

One of our friends, sneaking off to buy champagne to celebrate our escape from Kabul, abruptly interrupted our joyful reunion, saying "These Pakistanis are crazy!" "How can they say that?" In the shop where he had asked for a bottle of bubbly, the salesman had exclaimed: "Ah, you too are celebrating Bin Laden's victory! I'm out of champagne, I've sold it all, we're all so happy!"

We too had heard bursts of laughter and thunderous declarations expressing the joy of the successful attacks. We also knew that over 10% of the Pakistani population supported the Taliban and other terrorists, but still. . .

The leaden atmosphere suddenly brought us back to the awful reality—the horror of the attacks in the U.S. kept us from fully savoring the relief of simply being alive.

Part Five: The Pelican

Chapter Twenty-Six

The Hatching

The sadness of returning to France under these conditions matched my impatience to go back to Kabul. But Jacques, as always, calmer and wiser than me, reminded me of reality. Without a project, without a place to live, and without a visa, things would be very complicated.

"We must wait for the Taliban to be definitively driven out of Afghanistan and pray that there will not be too many deaths among the population. Only then will we return, Ariane."

I sighed.

"And," he commented, "let's take advantage of this time of rest and recreation to get some air and see our friends! We're very tired and have been under a lot of stress lately, I think it would be good to relax. I'll go golfing and you can come with me on the greens to change your melancholy into gratitude for the beautiful landscape. How long has it been since we admired this range of greens? We'll feel like we're walking on the most luxurious carpet in the softest shades. Finally, in the evening, I'll take you out for a good sauerkraut with a glass of crémant!"

To that... I agreed!

To persuade me even more, he added with loving eyes shining with hope, "You could take advantage of this time to work on the description of our project to help the street children of Kabul."

I gave him a broad smile: he had convinced me!

His logical plea hit the nail on the head, and I knew he was right. I admired his calmness and his ability to bounce back from the most difficult, sometimes even dangerous, situations. I marveled at his never-failing faith, leaning on that unshakable rock he had found in God; he feared nothing and no one.

This solid, deep, confidence that Jacques drew from regularly reading the Scriptures gave him conquering strength. His ambition to follow the Lord gave him wings. In his youth, trying to win in all his sports, he always aimed for first place on the podium. Likewise, his faith in Jesus further stimulated this character trait and naturally led him to become a winner in life.

I got to work writing down the details of the project, addressing the specific needs of poor children in Kabul. We often discussed it, and Jacques took on the administrative and financial elements. We looked for people who would agree to join us in this adventure.

Our priorities were to aid the Hazaras, the discriminated-against ethnic group, and to help the younger generation. It was therefore necessary to plan for a long-term project because we knew it would take many years to improve the living conditions of this community. Although there was a range of emergency programs, they were insufficient to make up for the critical deficiencies the Hazaras had suffered. We wanted to work with them for a long time. The experience of previous assignments had shown us that planning and working for the long term is necessary because bringing light and hope takes time. Moreover, assisting a naturally suspicious population, because they had so often been ostracized, would not be easy.

The fox in Saint-Exupéry's *Little Prince* often came to mind. Like him, I told myself that it was necessary first "to create links" and that winning them over would only be done under these conditions. Walking on tiptoe so as not to frighten those who had suffered so much seemed the very least we could do, and we knew that even love and goodwill would not be enough in cases of extreme suffering.

After two months of rest, good Alsatian cuisine, golf, walks, family dinners and parties with friends, we began to soften. The haggard eyes of the little Kabulis and their unwashed faces frequently arose in the course of general conversation. Their frail shadows searching for food and begging for notebooks and toys haunted me day and night.

So I finally saw the sky clear up when Jacques said, "Ariane, do you still want to go back to Kabul?"

It was, of course, a rhetorical question since my dear husband knew perfectly well my burning desire and my fondest dream was to take care of the vulnerable children of Afghanistan. How dare he even ask me such a question?

But I played along and smiled, knowing that if he asked, it certainly was not for nothing and that he must have a plan! Indeed, the rest of the hopeful sentence lit up his teasing smile, "Here we are too good, and as our English friends say, too comfortable. We've had enough rest, don't you think? And I'm gaining a lot of weight, which is not good for my health. I've been thinking…"

But yes, he had a clever strategy, my Jacques! And that's what we were going to do: create our own organization.

"And I came up with a name: The Pelican! What do you think?"

On the golf course, in that beautifully peaceful, green expanse, Jacques often spoke to the Creator. Later I understood that, on the course, he had gratefully welcomed the inspiration from above. A challenge was offered to us.

And that's how the first page of the Pelican's story was written.

Was this crazy project an indication of our naivety, or, on the contrary, was it a sign of our faith in action? Finally, was this God's response to our dedication to His work that we had affirmed, together as a couple, a few years earlier? For like the children of Israel in the wilderness, *"moved in heart and willing,"* *(Exodus 35:21),* we boldly submitted to what we believed to be God's desire.

Only time would tell…

★★★

As the creation of a humanitarian organization takes time, we sent our CVs to two French NGOs to quell our impatience. While most of them were hesitant to resume their activities in Afghanistan, we received a favorable response from one and were summoned to Paris to meet the management there.

On the train back to Colmar we dreamed of our next departure for the country where we had left pieces of our hearts. Indeed the interview with the directors left no doubt about their decision to send us to Kabul. And while we drove, reassured, towards Alsace, we soberly reflected on all that we would soon no longer be able to do.

For me: returning to Afghanistan meant no more freedom. It would be impossible to drive, dress in European style, go shopping, or drink a Coke on the terrace of a café. I would have to forget my spirit of independence!

For Jacques, it meant no more golf, or cold beers after his favorite sports lunches with friends. No more long showers with the inexhaustible water jet, no more dinners out with me in a restaurant of his choice, no more surprises, and certainly no more ... open evangelism!

We were saying goodbye to all those little things that give life a little spice, comfort, and happiness, those simple joys, light and transparent like champagne bubbles.

But we would gain so much in exchange: the smiles and laughter of the children, the progress of their education, their tenderness, their beautiful faces full of hope, and their licorice-colored eyes often wrinkled with mischievous grins!

And once we had filled their bellies and dressed them warmly, they would come to trust us, and then we would have won the greatest bet: to bring the Love of God, in the name of Christ. No, we would never be frustrated. No, we would never have any regrets because it was the right choice. It would become our joy.

Before leaving France, Jacques had planned a visit to our friends from the Bible School in England: Véronique and Paul. At the time, they lived in Lorraine where they had accepted a pastoral position a few years earlier. We counted on their spiritual support and wanted to share our new life project with them. The intercession of this church of which Paul was the pastor would be indispensable in keeping us off the wrong path, we who so needed the wisdom from on High!

At the end of the weekend, as we said goodbye, Véronique asked us a crucial question: "If you start this organization, have you thought about giving it a name?"

"Yes," Jacques replied softly, his eyes shining and his voice deep. "The Pelican."

Both surprised by this choice and elated by the knowledge she had of the historical comparison of the pelican with Christ, our friend jumped up from her chair. Meeting Jacques' gaze, she could not restrain her enthusiasm. We had to go follow our hearts, it was a sign from heaven!

When we learned that the bird had long been a symbol of Christ, even though Jacques had chosen the name for its neutrality, we were effectively convinced of the presence of the Lord at the head of this future NGO. Our friends were right: this name was inspired.

We needed to know more about this metaphor. Our readings led us to discover an Arabic legend reported by Saint Augustine, one of the founding fathers of the early church. A father pelican, having inadvertently killed his three babies, sprinkled them with his blood and the babies came back to life!

Later, the book our friend told us about, entitled *The Pelican: Story of a Symbol* (Paris: Editions du Cerf, 1984) would hold a place of pride in our library and we would take it along on the organization's presentation tours. Indeed, this unusual name would prompt many questions among people attending the conferences. In his writings, the author describes pelicans found in religious paintings of the Middle Ages, but also adorning chalices, cathedral squares, tabernacles, and baptismal fonts. Imagine our amazement when we found ourselves in a Mennonite church near Mulhouse, facing a bas-relief adorned with a pelican! While discovering the various representations of the pelican through the ages and other legends, we joined the author in his astonishment, "the pelican, an impure bird in the Bible, had become an image of Christ, representing an astonishing work of imagination over the centuries."

This bird symbolized the remission of sins, but it was above all Lucienne Portier's explanation, strangely resembling our own story, that moved us the most: "God creates men for their happiness; they rise up against him and hurt his love; they are thus dead to grace. Merciful God raises them up through the blood of his crucified Son. Hence the legend: the pelican plays happily with its chicks who strike it, it kills them, then mourns them and resurrects them with the blood of its own chest."

God spoke to us through the name of the pelican, and it was up to us to take up his offer or obey him.

If this common name lent itself well to living in a fundamentally Islamist country, it also reminded us of our old passion to fly like birds. Finally, the father pelican bringing food to his children represented exactly what the organization was going to achieve: to feed the spirit through education and also fill hungry stomachs! I thought back to the phrase from my Latin class that perfectly expressed what we wanted to accomplish: "*Mens sana in corpore sano.*" A holy spirit in a healthy body.

Finally, the words of the Apostle Paul touched on our last hesitations: "*What, then, shall we say in response to these things? If God is for us, who can be against us?*" (Romans 8:31)

We would therefore establish the NGO and go where the Spirit led us.

In February 2002, a week before we departed for Kabul, to work with the humanitarian organization headquartered in Paris, the creation of the Pelican association was registered at the Colmar district court. The Mennonite Church, of which we had been members since 1999, got involved immediately. After an evening informational meeting held on its premises, the organization of Le Pelican was formed. Seven volunteers were recruited that evening and almost all are still involved to this day. May they be warmly thanked here for their loyalty, generosity, trust, and friendship. Once again, the Lord had opened hearts and aroused enthusiasm, creating a momentum that has not diminished since that date.

Mennonites are extremely generous, and churches support many mission projects around the world. We had no idea how engaging and encouraging they would be for us. In fact, at the time of our return to

God, we were not familiar with the various Protestant churches and knew nothing of this evangelical church whose building was in our Alsatian village.

In the beginning, just after our conversion, Willy Petterschmitt wanted to integrate us into his Mennonite church, but we were Pentecostals at the time and declined his invitation. When we first entered the Mennonite church building in 1999, I gladly knew that Willy, finally satisfied and already in paradise, was certainly smiling down on us!

Discreet and warm at the same time, the members of this community welcomed us with great sensitivity. Respecting my silences and our quick escapes at the end of the service, no one bothered us or tried to hold us back with untimely attention.

Friendly and smiling, they practiced an unadorned devotion, which suited us perfectly. Coming from a Pentecostal church, we found the atmosphere calmer and the ambient rigor encouraged us to meditate and pray. But it was above all the preaching based on the Word of God that thrilled us.

A dinner invitation given one Sunday by one of the families of the church certainly remained the most striking memory of this time in our lives.. At the end of that afternoon, our car's GPS led us to a large building in a small village fifteen kilometers from Colmar. The yard, cluttered with tractors, vats, and other equipment, clearly demonstrated the work of the owner. Further on in a barn, about twenty cattle with bewildered eyes were quietly digesting their ration of feed.

Without fences or gates, the large space surrounded by the house and the sheds immediately appealed to us with its rustic and modern atmosphere, active and orderly. A mixed smell of earth, plants, and animals floated everywhere and made me think of my childhood when I cycled along the paths bordering the fields.

When the door was opened by the farmer gentleman, he greeted us with a huge smile, his powerful arms crushing Jacques against his broad chest. I immediately thought of one of the patriarchs of the Bible. This new friend, Daniel, had an imposing appearance and a full beard, but above all, he exuded the solid faith of Moses, who led the Israelites across the Red Sea, following God who traced a dry path while holding back the raging waters.

While his determined bearing might have seemed authoritarian, very quickly the softness of his gaze revealed a very sensitive heart. And when, in the evening breeze, we heard him say "Welcome friends" in a jovial and already affectionate voice, we felt unconditionally welcomed. His wife, just as warm, immediately ushered us into the house, filled with the enticing aromas of a carefully prepared meal. Jacques' appetite would no doubt be quite satisfied that evening! From then on, busying herself in the kitchen to shower us with delicious food, Laure, radiant under her brightly colored apron, surprised us with her: "Thank you, Lord, thank you Lord!" exclaimed in a cheerful voice. We were amazed by such an effusive demonstration of gratitude for a perfectly cooked pie.

We enjoyed dinner in a friendly and relaxed atmosphere. Then, to our great delight, their children improvised a concert. One on the violin, another on the flute, and a third on the piano. The young people of this house turned out to be not only charming but also talented musicians. Finally, to close the evening, Daniel grabbed a big black book with a threadbare cover and read us a passage from the Bible. Then prayers went up to God in all simplicity. From that day on, a deep friendship began that has never waned.

On the way back through the beautifully moonlit countryside, Jacques and I, still under the spell of the evening, remained silent. Each of us relived the details of that moment. We were struck by the faith and the honesty of this family who refused any compromise leading them away from the Bible. Daniel and Laure embodied Jesus' prayer to his Father before leaving the world. *"My prayer is not that you take them out of the world, but that you protect them from the evil one."* (*John 17:15*) We admired this couple because they demonstrated the demands of the gospel through their everyday actions, and we understood that Jesus' demands were achievable even in our time, despite the headwinds.

Attracted by the radicalism of the Gospel that the Mennonites seemed to live, we wanted to know them and understand their origin and their history. A brochure taken from the foyer of the church in Ingersheim introduced us to the first rudiments of this movement, unknown in France, but popular in the United States.

In the mix of denominations resulting from the Reformation, the Mennonites are certainly not very well known. But just as we speak of Lutherans in memory of Luther, or of Calvinists in memory of Calvin, the Mennonites take their name from Menno Simons, a Dutch reforming priest (1495-1561) who tried to organize the radical wing of the Protestant movement. This movement had enjoyed great success among the popular masses and extended from Switzerland to Holland, but was later severely repressed, both by the political and religious authorities of the time.

The true origins of this movement lie in Switzerland around the 1520s. In Zurich, the Reformation initiated by Zwingli experienced its own upheavals: deep differences appeared between reformers on certain points such as the separation of church and political power, the use of violence, or the practice of baptism.

Those whose careful consideration had led them to positions deemed too radical were dubbed "Anabaptists." Persecuted, they emigrated to Germany, Alsace, the Pays de Montbéliard, and Holland, where the authorities were willing to welcome them, and then to other continents.

Since 1945, the M.C.C. (Mennonite Central Committee), one of the world's leading humanitarian organizations, has served in all areas of conflict and disaster around the world, without condition and regardless of race, religion or politics.

None of these details make it possible to associate these splinter groups of the Reformation to any of the spurious sects which hit the headlines, even if the reputation of fundamentalism, which is sometimes used to describe them, forms certain stereotypes in the mind of the public.

We completely recognized ourselves in the motto of Émile Kremer, the late Mennonite preacher: "Believe, Want, Decide, and Pay the Price."

Chapter Twenty-Seven

First Flight

After four months away, returning to Kabul in the middle of winter in 2002 filled us with unique emotions. Mixed with the joy of returning home was the worry of what we would discover. We had watched the Taliban debacle and the joyful chaos that followed on television. The Afghans rejoiced at being able to shave since the exposure of any beardless man's skin was forbidden under the rule of religious fanatics. As for the women, they often "forgot" their burkas, and many wore only a simple veil. Schools were now filled with throngs of laughing children proudly holding an old book and a few sheets of paper. It was so gratifying to see Kabul in turmoil with a hopeful future opening up. With naïve optimism, we also looked forward to a time of lasting peace and reconstruction.

Afghans from the diaspora were returning en masse to help their country, many of whom had left when the Russians invaded. They had fled when they were very young and had never returned to the land of their ancestors. Their Dari or Pashto, the two main Afghan languages among the thirty-two dialects, were sometimes rudimentary. Having become Americans or Europeans in their culture, their education, and their way of behaving, these natives had great difficulty integrating back into their own country.

Their return was tough because the culture shock was very real. Arriving full of hope, they now found that their nation had become another world; they did not recognize their homeland. The Afghanistan their parents talked about no longer existed. The Russian invasion and then the civil war had given way to the most closed Islamic republic in the world.

And although the Taliban had gone, it would take a long time to bring some levity to the heavy silence.

Disappointed and sad, the new arrivals observed with amazement the endemic corruption plaguing the country up to the highest echelons of government. The market economy was dying. The flickering electricity only illuminated the neighborhoods where prominent Afghan figures lived, with the rest of the city plunged into total darkness as soon as the sun disappeared. In this gloomy context, newcomers also discovered the horror of children wearing plastic sandals, wandering in the snow, and looking for something to eat. So, some of them, for the first time on Afghan soil, revolted before the crying misery of their compatriots and sought to fight against it. Others, embarrassed and sad, revealed to us that they would never have imagined this situation and did not hide their disillusionment.

And because they hadn't seen, as we had, hanged men swinging sinisterly from the end of a crane in Ariana Square, because they hadn't heard the screams of women or children being whipped by an angry Taleb, or been assaulted by Kalashnikovs and cudgels wielded by turbaned fanatics, and, above all, because they had been absent and warm in their adopted countries, these disappointed Afghans did not survive their trial period in Kabul.

So, they left looking sad and guilty and promising to return, but most never did. We met several of these engineers, doctors, and lawyers whose intelligence and excellent educations would have helped their country so much. We tried to convince them to stay but without success.

What a shame to see them leave, even if we understood their reasons, we who were immersed in this mess. It takes a little madness and real motivation to live in Afghanistan. You have to have a strong heart and a stiff backbone to stay there for a long time. Honestly, during especially hard times, I sometimes still wonder to myself, if only for a moment, "What am I doing here?"

But I have long understood that the real questions are, "What more can I do? What can I do better? How can I love them more?"

And I know I still have a lot of work to do!

⋆⋆⋆

We had signed a one-year contract with the NGO EMDH (Enfants du Monde, Droits de l'Homme, or Human Rights for Children of the World). Jacques was head of mission and I was the administrator, to set up the organization's office in Kabul and create a reception center for vulnerable children. As I visited the families, I quickly realized that some of them were dying of exhaustion and hunger. Some children could no longer walk because of chronic malnutrition. Based on this observation, we asked the President of Le Pelican in France to organize a collection in the church so that we could feed needy families. Although still working for EMDH, this was our first action on behalf of the Pelican in Afghanistan.

Every month, I brought rice, oil, sugar, tea, and red beans to the families who had been waiting for our car since dawn. As soon as they saw us, the relieved mothers knew that their offspring and husbands would eat their fill again that day. The calories from the nutritious meals gave the fathers strength and confidence to go out and find a job. For their part, the children, without stomachs aching and swollen with just bread and water, slept peacefully until morning. Twenty-one families received food for six months. During this period, I observed that the Hazara children bounced back exceptionally in the face of the various traumas they had experienced. They did not particularly need psychological help, but rather a full belly.

The choice to support the Hazara population had also been discussed at length with the NGO management who did not understand our preference. So, when one of the managers came to check on the project, I immediately took her to visit families in the neighborhood. "Ariane, you were right, they are really poor. I understand now why you insisted on establishing the center in the Hazara quarter. You are definitely among the most vulnerable in Kabul."

The Afghan government authorities registered Le Pelican and authorized it to operate in the country. So naturally, we declined the proposal to renew our contract with the Parisian agency for a second year. We would now work only on behalf of the Pélican.

The experience of creating a center for children in the Hazara neighborhood taught us much and saved us from making the mistakes that other organizations sometimes made. Yet a new anxiety hovered in our minds: we did not know what really awaited us because we no longer benefited from the security of being employed by an international NGO. No house or car at our disposal and just enough money to support our daily life and possibly start a mini project. The future seemed more than uncertain and unpredictable.

A year earlier, we had left Kabul confused and sheepish. We were now back with the hope of a new beginning, finally solidifying our desire to help our favorite ethnic group, as long as possible. The 25,000 euros essential to our trip was already a miracle and I am always full of gratitude to the people who so generously answered our call. Without these charitable hearts, the Pélican project would never have seen the light of day.

Dr. Martin Luther King Jr.'s phrase often comes to mind when I think of those days: "You don't have to see the whole staircase, just take the first step." We didn't know if there would even be a second step, or if it would be so rickety our project would collapse into nothingness. But we continued to believe in the One who placed them under our feet, who rectified their height and consolidated their structure. I still can't see the last step, but I firmly believe I will reach it one day and that another life will then open up, bright and eternal, without any difficulties.

Chapter Twenty-Eight

Miracles

I remember that first day so well. We opened wide the doors of the Pelican school, and our hearts even more. Overwhelming joy filled my entire being! I would finally fulfill the commitment I had made three years earlier! I saw the children arrive with their yellow complexions and almond eyes opened wide. Their sad smiles reminded me of the kids I had seen rummaging through garbage piles in the days of the Taliban.

The barbarians had left Kabul just two years earlier. The Hazara came back to the country little by little. They finally came out of their hiding places in the Hazarajat mountains and left the neighboring countries of Pakistan and Iran.

The creation of the first center at the very end of the Hazara neighborhood was a miracle, and our address, "End of the Road," indicated the geographical isolation in which we found ourselves. The comments of other expatriates made us smile: "They are at the end of the world, literally and figuratively!"

Our immersion into the population led us to better understand the needs, the sufferings, and the aspirations of this place. We wanted to quench this thirst for justice and replace discouragement with hope. We aimed to give young people something approaching a normal childhood, with education, meals, and games, all of which they had been deprived of for many years.

The year 2003 saw the arrival en masse of "returnees" (Afghans who had fled their country and then returned) pouring into reception camps, organized by the United Nations. We observed entire families huddled together on carts laboriously pulled by donkeys or scraggly horses. Men with weathered skin and gaunt faces cast a vague gaze over the ambient misery. On the carts or in the trunks of the cars, the women, dazed by an interminable journey with multiple dangers were submerged in an opaque silence. Only the babies were screaming with hunger and thirst.

Their abruptly abandoned villages had been ravaged and burned by the Taliban before they had been driven out. Faced with their probable defeat, they had worked to do as much harm as possible before their departure and had competed in cruelty.

So, crossing the threshold of the Pelican for the first time, the families and their children probably had the impression of entering paradise, they, who had just arrived from hell. Some, traumatized by the dramas that would haunt their memories for a long time, slowly let themselves be vulnerable. It was at this time that, overwhelmed by their experiences, we thought of recording their stories. (They were compiled into a book, *Hearts to Heart,* published in English in 2012.)

We experienced small miracles daily, counting only on God. We entrusted our day to him each morning, asking for his blessing. Hungry for encouragement, we also needed the protection of the Most High.

One evening, Jacques felt very ill and went to bed immediately. He had been coughing for a long time, but we blamed it on the dust and pollution of Kabul. So when I took his temperature and the thermometer read over 104 degrees, I knew I had to act! The earth seemed to give way under my feet as I understood the danger. Alone in the night, at the end of nowhere, with Jacques, who was now delirious, how was I going to get out of this? Desperate, I was shaking all over. So I cried out to the Lord to help me, to inspire me, and I begged Him to intervene and reduce the fever.

As quick as lightning, an idea popped into my mind, despite my panic. I remembered my little boy at the hospital in Paris, where the nurses, unable to bring his temperature down, had used an ice-cold hot water bottle. Then, in the most absolute darkness, I groped for the small generator-powered refrigerator which kept a few drinks cool. I grabbed the first bottle and tried to refresh Jacques by applying towels soaked in the liquid to strategic places to bring down the fever.

I repeated the operation several times during the night. I didn't notice anything special except that Jacques seemed a little sticky, probably due to the fever. When the day broke, bringing me the hope of finally getting help, I discovered bottles of soda at the foot of the bed instead of bottles of water that I thought I had used: my husband of such a tender nature also became very sweet under my care!

A few days earlier, by chance, a Canadian colonel had handed us his business card in case we needed medical help. I called him at 5:00 a.m. and we went there immediately. A few minutes later the diagnosis came: Pneumonia that had nothing to do with the pollution and dust of Kabul!

The next day, at dawn, the head doctor told me, "So far, your husband is responding well to the antibiotics. Hopefully, in twenty-four hours we will have confirmation. Leave him now, he is very tired. You came just in time! My colleague explained your work to me, but your lives are also precious. If you want to continue helping Afghans, watch out. And bring back vitamins and dietary supplements from France. Eating only rice does not strengthen the immune system."

Then shaking my hand, he wished me good luck.

"Thank you and good luck to you too Colonel, you need it too!"

The Canadian Army was an important part of ISAF (International Security Assistance Force) and their soldiers served with courage and determination to restore order after the departure of the Taliban. Many of them did not return home and spilled their blood on the Afghan soil they had come to pacify.

Our gratitude to God went up because this doctor had undeniably saved Jacques' life. *Chance* had facilitated the contact since without the business card we would not have had access to the camp. In his omniscience, the Lord knew and foresaw, and in his grace, he provided. The care of God and his providence have never failed us.

At that time, we used to treat ourselves after our busy days to an aperitif consisting of orange juice accompanied by a host of dried fruits. We savored these moments of relaxation and intimacy on the toshaks, (large Afghan cushions) placed on the floor in a corner of the living room. I then crawled towards Jacques and curled up against his body, to capture the tenderness and the security which I always had an immense need of, even after thirty years of marriage. I loved these moments, and I let myself imbibe energy and strength from his being.

But one evening, a searing pain in his abdomen overwhelmed him and despite many painkillers, he suffered excruciatingly until dawn. When at the first glimmers of light, I discovered the olive-green color of his face, I immediately understood the gravity of the situation.

This time, we went to the Jalalabad Road military camp where the main international forces were located, including the French. An ultrasound revealed his gallbladder was filled with large stones, one of which obstruct-ed the bile duct, putting Jacques in danger of death if he did not have immediate surgery.

"The French surgeon specializing in this type of operation left today, and no one can replace him. I'm sorry… I can't do anything except lessen the pain," a female doctor explained to me. "We need a miracle." I was speechless, dazed with shock. Jacques was put on a camp bed next to wounded soldiers.

It was January and it gets dark very quickly during the winter in Kabul. Moreover, I could not go out after the curfew. So defying all shyness and arming myself with audacity, I asked Irene, the doctor in question, for permission to stay on the base. With a dubious pout, the young woman stammered that she would go and ask her colonel. "We can't just kick you out of camp and leave you on the road all alone with night falling and bombs exploding!" she whispered. Dear Irene, there is no doubt that she pleaded with her leader with determined compassion.

Sitting on Jacques' bed, I suddenly saw a bed arrive, followed by a dinner that I did not touch, despite the beautiful pink ham whose flavor I had not tasted for a year. The soldier next to me, to whom the nurse had told of Jacques' disastrous state, looked at me with pity and motioned for me to eat to regain strength. The kindness of the German soldiers encouraged me as with modest smiles they revealed, beyond their roughness and their uniforms, the grace of human beings, and their capacity to be moved by the suffering of another.

Jacques, exhausted but freed from his pain, fell asleep innocently, unaware of the seriousness of his condition and the impossibility of dealing with it.

I must have dozed off for a few minutes, when out of nowhere, I saw a shadow at the same time as I felt pressure on my arm. Leaping out of bed, I found myself face to face with a French soldier who said softly, "I am the anesthesiologist, my colleague, the gastrointestinal surgeon and I were to leave this morning, but a last-minute breakdown prevented the plane from taking off. The mechanics struggled with repairs all day without success, so we returned to camp. I am aware of your husband's condition. Don't worry, we will operate on him tomorrow morning. I gave orders; the room is ready. You need to sleep; I brought you some pills that will relax you."

"Ah, these doctors and their pills," I thought quickly. But these had been given with tact and had nothing to do with the exasperated rejection of Frantz's doctor twenty years before. I did not take the pills in question but thanked God. It was the miracle requested by the kind Irene without any trace of hope. The conundrum with which I had been struggling since the day before loosened at this precise moment, and I fell asleep next to Jacques.

The next morning the surgeon reassured us, "The dangerous stone went away naturally. There will be no operation, but you must return to France as soon as possible for further treatment. Contact your insurance to request emergency repatriation."

The next day, a private jet took off from Paris to look for the patient, Jacques Hiriart. At Kabul airport, with untimely zeal, the police officers asked us for authorizations which, of course, we did not have. Thinking they were dealing with spies, like in the Soviet era, they suspected Jacques of faking an illness to flee illicitly! Seeing my dismay, the chief pilot walked me into the office and said, "Don't worry, we'll be leaving. If they continue to fuss with us, I will come out, follow me and on my signal, run and get on the plane. My colleague knows how to do it, he will hit the throttle and we will take off immediately. We've done it before, don't worry!"

Oh good! But what movie were we starring in?

Half an hour later, to my great relief, the sinister-looking officers granted the departure authorization without even having to be bribed, and we took off. When, high above Kabul, I saw the houses disappear, I sighed, finally reassured, we were flying to France.

Jacques, under the effects of morphine, dozed and didn't worry about anything, well wedged in his seat which prevented him from moving. Bewildered, I let myself be carried away by events that were completely beyond me. Bringing Jacques to a proper hospital where he would be treated and cured belonged to the Miracle Maker. About two hours later, we landed in Baku, the capital of Azerbaijan, where a splendid Slavic pin-up girl was waiting for us on the tarmac, straight out of an OSS 117 film! In charge of checking the flight plan, the young woman dressed and made up in the latest fashion made a strong impression on me, coming from the land of burkas and gray silhouettes. I looked for James Bond to appear, elegant and handsome, a dry martini in his hand, smiling irresistibly.

Lying on an extended seat, I saw in a fog the orderly handing me a lunch tray: "And eat everything! This lunch cost us 40,000 euros!" he growled. I certainly didn't need his order after three days of dieting, so the most expensive meal of my life was devoured in the blink of an eye, and I enjoyed every bite of it!

Night was falling when we landed in Colmar, where Marie-Laure, my brother-in-law Henri, Freddy, the President of the NGOm and his wife were waiting for us. An ambulance took Jacques directly to the hospital where he would be operated on eight days later.

These stories are part of the life of an expatriate in Afghanistan, and I believe it was not luck, as we have heard so often, but divine protection.

But why doesn't it seem to work for everyone?

Chapter Twenty-Nine

The Light Bringer

W e had signed up for the choir for the Easter celebration along with twenty others. At the end of the rehearsal, Jacques exclaimed, "These hymns are very similar to the ones we sing in our Mennonite church in Colmar!"

Wide-eyed, as if he had seen a Martian, a man with a graying beard chuckled, "I must be dreaming—you're French—*and* you're a Christian? And besides that, you're Mennonite? How is that possible?"

It seems that Americans often think France is the most pagan country in Europe.

The following week we were invited to the house of this friendly American, Al Geiser and his wife, Gladys. From then on, every Friday, the Geisers invited us for lunch.

During this period, a resurgence of attacks occurred. It was the summer of 2008. One afternoon Farouk, the Pelican's driver, had just dropped Jacques off at an Afghan office building when suddenly a bomb exploded nearby. Windows, doors, files, chairs, trays, and teacups, shattered as the sirens wailed outside. The still hot breath of the bomb engulfed the Afghans' shalwars (traditional Afghan clothes), and transformed them into blimps while Jacques' swollen jeans made him look like a character from Folon's drawings, ready to fly away.

I had no idea what was going on as I watched the big black cloud rise above Kabul. After a few minutes of agonizing silence, a phone call reassured me that Jacques and Farouk were safe and sound.

"We're still not going to be any more afraid than we need to be," Jacques exclaimed, still optimistic when he returned. "Death is part of life everywhere and in every country, we know it, but here it is the intimate companion that invites itself more regularly, that's all." And we resumed our usual routine.

When you decide to work in a country at war, where the medical infrastructure is precarious and the security uncertain, you accept being injured or dying senselessly, for lack of care. The possibility of being kidnapped or murdered by enemy bullets is also present. Risk-taking reminds us that God is sovereign and that it is only he who decides whether or not to let his workers die on Afghan soil.

We were going to learn this lesson through our friends, Al and Gladys Geiser. When we went to their house, their arms would open wide on the doorstep to receive us. During a time when we lived in an underground room, Al with a warm smile greeted us saying, "Welcome to our stinky friends! Before eating, wash!" He chuckled, ushering us into the bathroom where soaps, shampoos, towels, and a basin of steaming water were waiting!

Our friend Al, an outstanding electrician, often helped Jacques out. His ingenuity made up for the lack of "electricity" departments in Afghan shops. His wife Gladys, a retired teacher, taught the children of expatriates from a large Christian organization in Kabul.

Then one day, when he was going to check on one of his projects, Al was kidnapped with his Afghan associate, Shukur. Their work, which was to generate electricity through water turbines, immediately ceased and the villages fell back into darkness. Rescued by the U.S. Army six weeks after his abduction, Al was awarded a Certificate of Appreciation from the U.S. Army. Rewarded for having done good work in a hostile country, he never boasted of this recognition. This good, generous, and exuberant man demonstrated exceptional courage by his determination to return to Kabul after his kidnapping under this pretext: "If God delivered me, it was certainly not to end my life, in cushy Ohio, in my slippers!"

It was a very hot morning in our office in Dasht-e-Barchi when the mobile phone rang. I can still see Jacques answering and jumping up, turning white and breaking out in a sweat. A few seconds caused our whole world to stagger. The call was from Gladys, announcing unbelievable news. It was a cry for help, a cry of distress! I couldn't accept the news. Al was dead. Impossible, I told myself. It must be a mistake, he had an accident. And yet...

He and his Afghan friend had agreed to spend the night in the village where they had installed hydroelectric turbines a few kilometers from Kabul. On the way back, pursued by a car forcing them to cross a small bridge, they were stopped by Taliban, Kalashnikovs in hand. The two friends and their young co-worker were shot dead immediately.

Jacques and an American pastor took care of the essential administrative papers and washed the body. The "Light Bringer" would be no more! Extinguished by a bullet passing through his body on both sides. I was revolted and felt my anger and hatred for the Taliban increasing.

WHY?

Gladys, devastated, returned to the USA to live in the little wooden house that her dear husband had built for her, and to continue to serve lost and needy people.

As for us, there was only one place where we were really meant to be: Afghanistan. I still don't know how to explain the deep and almost visceral attachment to this country that is inhospitable in so many ways. One late afternoon, as the center emptied of the hubbub of children and we admired the last rays of the sun illuminating our giant sunflowers, Jacques' calm and reassuring voice rose in the sweetness of the evening: "You know Ariane, I have never felt so at peace with myself, or so well. For the first time in my life, I know that I am in the right place, with you, among the Afghans."

I thought so too. We were both in the right place and we thanked our Father for this immense grace. Then we discussed the possibility of dying on Afghan soil like our friend Al and the other expatriates buried in the English cemetery in Kabul. But we didn't care. That would be OK, if it came to pass, because we were thinking of leaving together.

Chapter Thirty

Stormy Weather

W hen the workers began to demolish the center's walls, I could not hold back my tears which mingled with those of the children. Our forced move was one of the biggest obstacles of this period. An obstacle that I did not want to believe.

However, in the government's urbanization plan, our street would be widened and become an important road leading to the northern city of Mazar-e-Sharif. The surveyors made it pass exactly through the middle of our center, which signaled its destruction.

Jacques had managed to find another property for the Pelican Center, but it hadn't been easy. The move to the new center was done in Afghan style. We had hired two men from the street to haul furniture, school supplies, and office equipment about a mile away. These movers used "karachis" (large wheelbarrows pulled by men), which they hauled with courage. I was ashamed to employ these men who did the work of beasts of burden. But when I saw their big smiles when they received double the normal pay, I understood that in this country, one should not burden oneself with misplaced guilt, and this was a way of helping the poorest. These two old, skinny men would likely have gone home empty-handed had it not been for Jacques' offer. Our Hazara neighborhood is very similar to the land of Jesus' time where men, standing in a square, wait long hours to be chosen for jobs.

The population of the neighborhood had flocked to the door of the center every day since it opened, and more families begged us to accept their children. They thanked us with a lot of emotion, sometimes tearfully, and told us that we were the only ones not to reject them. Without the Pelican, they said, there would be no education, and their children would be condemned to making carpets or doing other hard, manual jobs on the street. They would have no hope of improving their futures.

This had been the lot of the students' parents and they wanted a better life for their children. They understood the importance that education played in gaining a future brighter than theirs had been.

Our relationship of friendship with the Hazara people, begun in 2002, has never ceased and has turned into deep, faithful affection throughout the years. I think they understand that we simply love them.

Obstacles have always accompanied us over the years. They became wonderful pretexts for more grace and blessings from God, whom we felt was an active presence in our endeavors. Our faith, nourished by His Word and tested and strengthened by the difficulties of life in Kabul, always pushed us further in the help that we wanted to bring to the Hazaras. Jacques' enthusiasm did not wane, nor did my determination to accept more children.

It was 2005 and many events still awaited us on this path of life on which the Lord had been leading us since we had given ourselves to him. Sure of the love of the Father, the closeness of the Son, and the continual assistance of the Holy Spirit, a great peace dwelt in us despite all kinds of difficulties inherent in the country.

When we converted to Christ a few years earlier, we had made David's phrase our own: *"If the Lord delights in a man's way, he makes his steps firm; though he stumble, he will not fall, for the Lord upholds him with his hand."* *(Psalm 37:23,24)* Without Heaven's help and encouragement, we would have been struck down several times.

The troubles followed one another in a cascade, but the blessings too. In the train stations of my childhood, a sign often warned: "Attention, a train can hide another one!" So regularly, and with a disillusioned pout, I addressed myself to Jacques: "Be careful, one obstacle certainly hides another." But his reassuring voice made me choose optimism. "Let's stay calm and confident: the blessings are also on the way! You know very well that the Pelican is not Jacques and Ariane's project, but the Lord's. He's the boss and he's the one running the shop. If he wants our work to continue, he will find a solution. Let's read the Bible." Very often a verse would fill our hearts with a deep calm and again, we would decide to trust God completely. We experienced the growing power of faith in the testing of our impatient natures.

And yet every trial would reveal grace in disguise! So, who to believe, and what to believe? We chose to believe God and his promises and allowed ourselves to be strengthened and encouraged each morning by reading the Bible. On days of great anguish, we asked him to confirm or overrule the direction we planned to take.

How could we exist without the inspiration from above, and continue to live in Afghanistan, without this intense and regular communication with heaven? Daily prayers and the Word of God were essential to our actions. We realized even more the privilege of having a Father to son/daughter relationship with God, the Almighty! And we never took that advantage for granted, but viewed it as an extraordinary gift, a unique treasure that had to be seized and shared, if possible. In the land of Islam, it was difficult, but not impossible.

Nineteen years have passed since then and when I look back, I can only see the goodness of God, who, by his spirit, made us grow spiritually, and also designed beautiful encounters.

All these obstacles that were overcome almost supernaturally assured us that the Lord was with us. He was the master of the most difficult situations. We were experiencing what we knew of him: "*I am the vine; you are the branches. If a man remains in me and I in him, he will bear much fruit; apart from me you can do nothing.*" *(John 15:5)*

We especially understood that he was the boss!

Chapter Thirty-One

The Calm Before the Storm

Looking back over these years, I know that without God, his Son Jesus, or the Holy Spirit, our most faithful adviser, we would never have accomplished this long journey. How could we have struggled along without the hand of the Lord, the assurance of our Master's guidance, and he prompting of the Spirit?

Indeed, the trials were transformed into blessings and showed us the way forward. We felt like the employees of a master builder with a well-founded and precise plan. The conviction that our boss would not let his teammates down motivated and reassured us. So we hummed, "Count the Blessings of God," that song that Mr. Perrenoud sang in the Evangelical churches of France, and which applied perfectly to our difficult circumstances.

The first blessing at the beginning of the adventure had come in response to a purely material problem. We had managed to raise the money needed to begin our work in Kabul. God had opened the way for us. Once there, and after several other steps, we received funds from the Japanese Embassy to start the work of the Center.

The center had been running for two years when we heard the news of the road widening project, that would lead to the destruction of the school where over eighty children were thriving! Discouraged and on the verge of tears, I heard Jacques say, "Ariane, the Pelican project is not our project; it is God's project. Therefore, we will do everything possible, but the solution belongs to our boss."

Then came the second blessing: one afternoon, *by chance*, Jacques visited a spacious property in a state of disrepair. For some time now, he had been thinking about vocational training for teenagers but had put this program aside for lack of space. A leap of faith was asked of us because we did not have the money to undertake the necessary renovation work. Yet we signed the rental agreement anyway.

A few days after the signing, we happened to meet a visiting American who was interested in the work of the Pelican and asked to visit the center. The rest of the story is part of the wonderful providence of God. When he returned to the United States, this stranger transferred $20,000 to the Pelican's bank account in France.

This second, much larger property showed us once again that God often turns disasters into blessings. The opportunity to implement vocational training was finally made possible!

Education, fun, and sports activities as well as hot meals filled a void necessary for the proper development of the children. "But after that?" Jacques wondered, "Have you thought about their future?" We both believed that helping the younger generation prepare for their future was part of our mandate. And since Jacques, the oilman, had also learned to bake bread, he would put his skills to use in training our young students. This part of the project would not only give them a job but would greatly improve the economy of the families since the apprentices would receive a significant stipend.

The bakery workshop built of local bricks rose quickly at one end of the schoolyard. With the ceramic tiling of the walls and the floor laid, Jacques installed ovens and baking equipment generously financed by Christians in the Mennonite Churches in France.

The French Minister of Defense allowed the airlifting of the equipment to a military base in Kabul—free! It is certainly not common for a fledgling NGO to obtain such generous benefits!

As soon as the bakery was finished, the wonderful smell of croissants and French bread rose very early in the fresh morning air, as the apprentices, under the professional eye of Jacques, began baking well before dawn.

Then, carried by the wind, a strangely Parisian aroma fanned out, appealing to young and old.

My dreams still took me to the Middle East where I imagined Jesus and his disciples feeding the crowd with bread and spiritual food. More than two thousand years had passed since then, but in our day we distributed bread and the love of the Lord to the hungry Hazara children. *"Jesus replied, 'You give them something to eat.' They answered, 'We have only five loaves of bread and two fish—unless we go and buy food for all this crowd. (Luke 9:13)*

We were now well settled only a kilometer from the destroyed center and practically all the children had followed us to the new location. Parents in our new neighborhood kept knocking on the door from morning till night, seeking a place for their children. And although we were full as an egg, I could not refuse these kids with sad faces, whose eyes shone with hope as they entered the school.

It was about that time that, on returning from a trip to France, Jacques noticed cracks in the walls of the children's lunch room. These suspicious cracks plunged us into great dismay. The building could collapse in the next earthquake, a frequent event in Afghanistan. We had no choice—the dangerous building had to be evacuated immediately.

Again we knelt in prayer. What would become of all of our students? Where could we go this time? We didn't have the financial means to start all over again anyway, noted Jacques, discouraged for once. Two weeks passed with no solution, but then the third blessing gave us back our hope. God, influencing the heart of the Afghan owner, produced a miracle.

Qazi Daoud sipped tea in our office with the piercing gaze of an eagle as he observed Jacques with his shiny black eyes. He did not have the nicest reputation in the neighborhood. A draconian judge, this lawyer applied Sharia laws.

"Jacques," he began in a deep voice, "I respect you and consider you my brother. We're going to demolish the building and rebuild it. Tomorrow my son will come and lead the demolition team; then we will do what is necessary. And I ensure the financing of the whole operation. I don't want you to go! Your reputation in the neighborhood is excellent, and people often thank me for having you as tenants!"

When he left, we thanked our boss! Again, he had fixed a problem that, with all the goodwill in the world, we were unable to solve. So with eyes wet with tears and our hearts filled with peace of mind at being in the Father's hand, our glasses of Coke clinked happily together. We would continue to support the Hazaras in the same place.

Children and families watched closely as the building was demolished and rebuilt, and eagerly watched for signs of the school's reopening.

Kabul ex-pats made aware of the situation were amazed.

"We've never seen anything like it!" they exclaimed in the meetings.

"But it's normal when you're a *very dear son*," Jacques announced mysteriously, giving me a knowing wink which obviously only I understood.

This name of "very dear son" had indeed never left him. It had been given to him at the beginning of our spiritual search by a very old Catholic sister, having the gift of prophecy.

At that time we were part of a prayer group that organized a gathering to receive the Holy Spirit. At the end of the evening, Jacques and I, surrounded by all the others, grew even more impatient and moved in expectation of the Spirit of God. Just then, despite her great weakness, the little nun turned to Jacques and prophesied in a loud voice: "You are a very dear son to me." Then she quietly added, "I have a job for you in my vineyard."

Very close to Jacques, I noted his emotion, and with tears streaming down his face he suddenly lit up with overflowing joy! On the other hand, my attitude was quite different. "This good sister is crazy! She's gaga, let her go back to her convent," I thought to myself. "It's Henri, the winemaker, who works in the vineyards, not Jacques, who makes bread in his bakery!" And I wanted to get out of there as quickly as possible.

But it turned out that I was the ignorant one who didn't understand anything. Because Jacques was going to work a lot in the vineyards of the Lord: *"For the kingdom of heaven is like a landowner who went out early in the morning to hire men to work in his vineyard." (Matthew 20:1).*

Over time I learned to accept a God who never ceases to want to communicate with his children. But I still had much to learn because total surrender to my Heavenly Father required the intellectual effort of becoming a child again, a *sine qua non* ("a necessary") condition for entering the Kingdom of God: *"I tell you the truth, unless you change and become like little children, you will never enter the kingdom of heaven."* (Matthew 18:3)

At that time, the Christian gathering for foreigners in Kabul was without a pastor. Jacques agreed to join the leadership group with Bill Newbrander. Brought together by this work, the two men bonded and met several times. God's plan was coming together.

Very interested in our work, Bill asked us if he and his wife Nancy could visit the center when she joined him in Kabul. We can without exaggeration, speak of a deep friendship begun that day: "If, in the future, I can help an NGO, it is there in Dasht e Barchi, at the Pelican that I want to do it!" Nancy stated to Bill, in the car taking them back to town.

Nancy is the daughter of Kabul's first pastor, J. Christy Wilson. She and her two brothers were born in the Afghan capital. Her father and mother, Betty, came to Kabul in 1951 to serve as Christian workers there. Afghanistan was known as a closed country, forbidden to outsiders. The government of Pakistan secured its northern border at the Khyber Pass. There a sign put up by the Afghan government stated, "It is strictly forbidden to cross the border into Afghanistan." This sentence implied a death threat to anyone who dared to cross over to the other side.

The country, closed and hostile to any Christian work, was dangerous. Yet the Wilsons came there as pioneers, hoping to use every means at their disposal to serve the people and share the good news of the gospel with Afghans. To do this, Christy Wilson taught English at Habibia High School for five years. Then, knowing that he was a trained Christian pastor, the expatriates of Kabul asked him to become their pastor. With permission from the government, he did so.

Over their time there, the couple lived in four homes around Kabul, ending up in Karte Seh, a neighborhood with a Hazara majority. When one day Betty saw a young blind boy on the street; her heart ached for him, so she invited him to her home and began teaching him braille. Then another little blind boy arrived. And a third…and finally, a fourth! This is how she created the first school for blind children, which still exists in Kabul.

One winter morning, we saw a young man arrive at our gate. He wore glasses with unusually thick lenses. His unsteady gait immediately indicated his visual impairment. How surprised we were to learn that Mustapha, who had become a braille teacher, had been one of Betty Wilson's students thirty years before!

Nancy's heart, like that of her mother's, had a soft spot for the most disadvantaged. Our help to them was, for her, a natural extension of her mother's work. She very generously offered her help, which we gratefully accepted. She began with health lessons for apprentice bakers, then for older girls and women whose problems she understood well from having lived in Kabul in her youth. Coming to Afghanistan regularly for Bill's work in the healthcare, Nancy became an immensely useful and valuable volunteer for the Pelican. And then one day, she softly uttered a question that would take her even further in her commitment:

"What else can I do for you, Jacques and Ariane?"

Our three looks met and amazed, I heard my dear husband say with his inimitable and convincing smile, "If you would like to represent us in the USA, that would be wonderful!"

Nancy said she would pray about it. Another adventure was about to begin…

When Nancy accepted our offer, we knew the Pelican would grow, and with its wings more widely spread, it would soar even higher in the Afghan sky. And for fifteen years now, thanks to Nancy and her team, the French NGO has been financially strengthened by its branch across the Atlantic. From all corners of America arise prayers, and God needs no translator!

So how can we forget or obscure the hand of God in this project? As the author of a book we read early in our spiritual research said, "It takes a lot of faith to be an atheist."

Chapter Thirty-Two

Oriental Croissants

With the number of people seeking our help increasing every day, the Pelican spread its wings further to attempt to accommodate them all. Indeed, frustrated by having to turn away young girls and women for lack of space at the first center, we considered creating a second location that would have classrooms and also a sewing workshop. Thus, the difficulty arose once again of finding the funds, the physical space, and the right personnel.

But how to send away the women and girls brought by their fathers and husbands to our gate day after day? How to say no to a pleading father, "It's quite simple, if you don't take her, she'll make carpets until we marry her off!" Of course, I had to relent in the face of the stubbornness of these fathers who, although illiterate, seized at the chance of an education that would bring a better future for their daughters. And so, I would enter a new name on the waiting list, while hoping that our second school would open soon.

We fervently believed the "Pelican Banker" would open the floodgates of heaven to meet the demand to educate the neighborhood's female population. And as if by a miracle, the donations began to pour in: transfers, checks, and cash arrived regularly in the Pelican's beak to specifically support the future women's school. The generosity of the donors who would never see the beautiful, studious faces of these young women touched us deeply and encouraged us to launch this new project.

On the bakery apprenticeship side, success came little by little as lessons were learned and progress was made. Every morning, about fifteen apprentices, led by Jacques with a free baguette, learned how to make brioches, pains au chocolat, and golden croissants, whose puff pastry rivaled that of traditional bakeries in France. It must be said that the delicious, typically French products delivered to the four corners of Kabul, became the delight of nostalgic expatriates longing for gourmet breakfasts. The unexpected luxury of savoring these treats undoubtedly also satisfied a certain homesickness they were feeling.

The local population around us was also very aware of Jacques' effort to provide vocational training for young people. The families of the apprentices often expressed gratitude because their sons not only received salaries, but also continued their studies. In addition, we added health and intensive English lessons to the curriculum. Observing the happy and satiated faces of these young people, other students enthusiastically signed up for the next "baker" course.

During this time Jacques, an incomparable visionary, expressed the desire to go even further! It was a time of possibility and why not? It was a time when the future of Afghanistan seemed open and when we still allowed ourselves to dream.

Thinking that the country would eventually be pacified, he now wanted to create a café to teach food trades, He also hoped for an influx of tourists that would come someday to admire one of the most beautiful landscapes in the world. Skeptical, I forced myself to consider the possibility that the situation in Kabul might improve. So we started looking for a location for the café. After much research, Jacques found the ideal building which would become the *Pélican Café* of Kabul as well as the mini hotel for the hospitality training that he had dreamed about.

Visiting expatriates were immediately won over by the Pelican apprentices in uniforms worthy of the best bistros on the left bank of Paris. The young Hazaras looked handsome with their orange bow ties and their impeccable white shirts over striped trousers. Their irresistible smiles, the charming greetings of "Welcome Sir, Welcome Madam," their polite attitudes, and their flawless service certainly contributed to the success of the café and factored into the amount of their tips! The foreigners from

Kabul and the Afghans of the diaspora met at Jacques and Ariane's place. Truly captivated by this little corner of paradise amid the chaos, dust, and dirt of the Afghan capital in 2008, our regulars assured us of a wonderful reputation. Stepping into the café garden for the first time, everyone found the place marvelous as well as surreal, and they returned regularly with colleagues and friends.

On busy days, when all the tables and seats were taken, customers sat on the windowsills to enjoy salads, Croque-Monsieur, bowls of soup, Quiche Lorraine, and various pastries. This melting pot of different cultures reminded us of the friendly atmosphere of the Croissanterie in Colmar, and after lunch was served, we liked to chat with our friends or meet new people.

But nothing is ever taken for granted anywhere on this planet and in Afghanistan, this takes on a particularly pointed meaning. Indeed, everything can collapse from one day to the next, especially due to security issues.

And that was the case. Attacks and kidnappings multiplied, and expatriates no longer went outside. Not far from us, a young woman from the Christian expatriate community was shot dead while leaving a store. Also, around this time, a group of our friends from a Christian NGO were gunned down by the Taliban on their way back from Nuristan, a northern province where they had traveled to provide health care to remote districts. I had sold loaves of bread a few days before to one of them, Terry, who had promised to visit our project when he returned. But neither he nor the other friends ever came back, and the bread our apprentices baked was one of their last meals.

We bitterly noted a surge of unprecedented violence. So when we were secretly warned that the Pélican Café was targeted, we sadly decided to close it.

The cessation of this activity was an economic disaster for the apprentices, their families' sole breadwinners. But because our lives and those of our clients were in real danger, we did not waver in our decision, despite the insistence of the boys. The Afghans, fatalistic by nature, often overlook risks and reject with a resigned "Inshallah," "if God wills," the most elementary precautions.

Faced with the sadness of the young, unemployed apprentices, Jacques found a solution to continue their professional training and to ensure their wages. Since the café was gone, we would open a bakery shop in town! It was as simple as that, according to him. Indeed this man of action was never discouraged and did not let unforeseen events rule his life. At each obstacle, while I was demoralized, he, in contrast, was thinking up a new strategy.

"We'll have to find a well-placed location, start decorating again, and find new customers, and all for nothing," I stewed to myself, tired of always having to start all over again. I fully subscribed to the phrase of Afghans fleeing their own country: "There is nothing we can do here!" In Afghanistan, everything was too hard, too sad, too corrupt, too dirty, too chaotic, too difficult; everything was too much, a thousand times too much!

Where was the hope? Where was the light? We had lived in this Afghan land for nine years and I saw no progress. My thinking showed an obvious lack of faith because there had been improvements in many areas in recent years. But blinded by weariness, I saw nothing...

"Ariane, we're not going to give up, let's talk to the Lord," Jacques said, opening the Bible.

'Therefore, put on the full armor of God, so that when the day of evil comes, you may be able to stand your ground, and after you have done everything, to stand." (Ephesians 6:13)

I knew what that passage meant: you had to fight on your knees and not flinch. So in the prayer meetings, I raised my arms up high again, like lightning rods connected directly to heaven. We immersed ourselves even more in the Word of God to be uplifted, encouraged, and protected. I made the firm decision to completely close my heart to the evil one who wanted to bury me and make me give up.

I would now listen to Him who whispered: "I have loved you with an everlasting love; I have drawn you with loving-kindness. (Jeremiah 31:3) Eyes raised to the Light, we crossed the dark spaces with the assurance that we were not alone.

Chapter Thirty-Three

The Cage

In the summer of 2010, while on a trip to France, we had heard of a religious scandal taking place in Kabul, but did not yet know that our friend, Mossa, was at the heart of the affair.

The photo of the renegade and his television appearance unleashed a public outcry, giving free rein to denunciation, lies, and betrayal. A despicable plot against Christian Afghans, that had been planned for more than a year, turned out to be a success. From then on, a ruthless hunt began, and most fled to India—except Mossa.

Employed for fifteen years at the Red Cross hospital in Kabul, he had become one of its best prosthetists. Who could understand his amputee patients better than he? When he was a young commander, he had lost a leg in a minefield. Having become a Christian, he vigorously rejected the reasoning of certain mullahs who believed his handicap manifested the wrath of God. He was fearless despite the hostile environment. This prosthetist announced the love of Christ and used a completely different language.

Finding Mossa turned out to be a real obstacle course for us! Finally, after two months of searching, we found out where our friend was jailed. I will remember all my life the horror of our first visit to his prison. A fence separated visitors from the wild beasts that these men had become after months in prison. Screaming, gesticulating, belching sarcasm and oaths, these haggard ghosts, drunk with violence and frustration, circled like aimless puppets. We saw Mossa among these mad-eyed beings, making his way with difficulty despite the tripping, blows, spitting, and insults of the other prisoners. We met at the fence behind which, dazed, we watched him painfully advance.

I lowered my head and used my veil to wipe away my tears while Jacques tried to encourage his friend and find out how he was being treated. On the third visit, he passed us his bag of dirty laundry in which he had hidden a letter describing the atrocity of his situation: "Please get me out of here!" Whispering in Jacques' ear, our poor friend revealed to him that he was beaten by the prisoners and the guards, since the judge had ordered: "Beat him to death. He is unclean!"

We were overwhelmed by the suffering of Mossa, who had become the scapegoat of the prison. So we decided to move heaven and earth despite the big risks involved. We appealed to several embassies, as well as United Nations agencies specializing in defending human rights. But annoyed, we always heard the same answer: "This is a far too sensitive and very dangerous case. Stop your efforts immediately!"

I still have a very bitter taste from this period when we had to confront the abandonment of official institutions and the reluctance of the Christian community in Kabul. "What shocks me most is not the cruelty of the wicked, but the indifference of the good," said Dr. Martin Luther King, Jr.

We had to change our strategy. Since our efforts were stagnating in Kabul, we had to spread the word beyond Afghanistan, so we contacted Christian newspapers and then the international press. A chain of prayers was organized immediately. Finally, things started to move!

Mossa was transferred to a maximum security prison where he would no longer be abused. Housing the worst criminals on death row, this place granted no visitation rights except to a family member. We hired a cousin-visitor who would bring him a package from us every week.

The seasons followed one another as Mossa languished in prison. Then we heard about a tactic that had proven itself in Africa and we decided to try it. At our request, an extraordinary international chain of solidarity was set up where any person of goodwill could write to Mossa. Stunned by the result, we were also very touched by discovering the diversity of the cities that the letters came from, including Colmar. When we found drawings by children in our own Church in the mail, we were deeply touched.

Many of the envelopes contained Christian messages, some Bible verses had even been translated into Dari. Mossa, condemned because of the Good News, was brought out with his feet shackled. In front of this mountain of mail, the stunned guards asked him to read his letters aloud. The Lord certainly has a sense of humor!

But alas, Mossa was still languishing in his cell, where now an arctic cold turned the damp walls into sheets of ice. So, after eight months of suffering and loneliness, our friend, unable to take it any longer, demanded the death he had so often been promised. He also asked that television cameras film his hanging so that, with a noose around his neck, he could publicly declare before he died: "You can kill my body, but you cannot kill my soul because I belong to God, since his Son Jesus saved me."

We did not accept the idea of Mossa's death. Besides, Afghanistan would need him later. But while our friend was at the end of his pain, we, heartbroken, were at the end of our resources. What more could we do? Only a miracle would save Mossa!

In his last message, he wrote that he had begged Jesus to act, and he extraordinarily answered him. That evening, Mossa, more overwhelmed than ever, fell asleep shivering. In the middle of the night, a man wreathed in a dazzling light woke him up. The humble Hazara immediately acknowledged the Lord, knelt, and felt a hand on his shoulder. He heard a voice say, "Son, you won't be in this prison much longer, take heart!" Then the figure dressed in white disappeared

Melodious songs of extraordinary beauty seeming to emanate from the four corners of the earth accompanied his vision: "I had never heard such beautiful, harmonious songs. I don't know what language was used, but never in my life have I perceived these sounds and this music. I did not understand the words that intermingled in a melodious melody. It was like water, maybe gushing fountains or waterfalls...I can't put into words what

I was hearing. But I can say a feeling of joy and peace supernaturally came over me. And from that night on, I was never discouraged or sad…ever."

Sometime after this experience, he was assigned a cellmate with a very bad reputation: this Taleb, known for his brutality and his crimes, immediately provoked a violent altercation with the "apostate," and threatened him with death.

Around three o'clock in the morning, a pressure on his arm woke Mossa, who discerned in the darkness the dangerous individual sitting quietly at his side.

"Your Jesus appeared to me in a dream and spoke with authority these strange words: "Listen to what my servant Mossa has to say to you. And believe it because it's the truth."

With a smile as dazzling as his faith, the disciple of Jesus joyfully said, "Come my brother, I will tell you about the Son of God." The marvelous hope of a God saving the world instantly illuminated that gloomy cell.

Then more days passed…

There was no trial for Mossa, despite several round trips to the Supreme Court where, tied like a wild beast, chain around his neck, feet and hands bound, he waited several hours for a verdict which was never delivered to him. This affair caused an outcry in Kabul. The religious leaders as well as certain members of Parliament wanted this man to be hanged as soon as possible. President Karzai's silence revealed the weakness of the government, which would not risk acting against the fundamentalists.

Yet nothing was happening to free the prisoner, and his family was now in great danger. The neighbors openly showed their aggression. One night, they pushed Guljan, his terrified wife, to burn their Christian books and cassettes. The whole neighborhood that Mossa had so generously helped for years turned against this one who, in their eyes, had become impure. There was only one solution for the family: take flight to Pakistan.

It was late January 2011. After the Lord spoke to Mossa of a future change of situation, we waited with him for his deliverance—or his execution. Was it a release on earth or a welcome to heaven? How should we understand the enigmatic sentence of Jesus?

Then, everything happened very quickly. The good news finally came in the middle of the night, "Your friend will be released in a few days, but don't tell anyone." On February 11, 2011, Mossa flew to Europe on a private jet, worthy of the most powerful on earth. "He too must have felt like a very dear son," Jacques said to me with a broad smile.

"This battle was fought by the Lord, he and he alone pulled Mossa out of the jaws of the enemy. To him, be all the glory," Jacques prayed, on his knees.

After this joy came the worrying question of reuniting the family, still in Pakistan. But to get them back across the border into Afghanistan was like a kidnapping because transporting Afghans without passports or visas could create big diplomatic problems if the secret was revealed. "You take care of bringing the family back and housing them in Kabul, and as soon as I have their identity papers I will request a plane for their evacuation," the secretary of an embassy ordered us.

When they arrived, Jacques asked for the taskéras (Afghan identity cards).

"Ah…Where are they?" said the mother.

"I don't know," the girls answered. "But it was you who had kept them, during the trip."

"Ah…Ah! They're in the plastic bag that was left in the car!"

Distraught, Jacques added, "And the car left."

Shock, disappointment, dismay! No papers meant no leaving this country and no reunion with their father in Europe. I prayed, "Lord, do something!"

"Don't panic, I have the taxi's cell phone, I'll call him," the Afghan in charge of the trip said calmly.

A quarter of an hour later, snatching the documents from the hands of the bewildered driver, Jacques immediately bolted for the embassy.

In the evening, sitting by the dinner laid out on the floor, the children, hands turned towards the sky, faces contemplative, asked Jesus to bless the meal. The smaller one raised his thin voice and also thanked God for the trip.

The embassy had planned to evacuate the family the next day. When at dawn, an anonymous phone call informed us, "They are in the air," we could finally breathe a sigh of relief!

From this period, I want to only remember the good: the release of Mossa and his family.

For nine months, terrified by the enormous risks, I had hesitated to jeopardize our project and perhaps our lives.

"Seriously, Ariane, could you look in the mirror every morning and sit idly by and do nothing? No, you couldn't! I know you." Seizing the sheet of the Christian calendar, Jacques exclaimed, "Hey, listen to this! I believe this is your answer: *"Therefore, as we have opportunity, let us do good to all people, especially those who belong to the family of believers."* (Galatians 6:10). God had spoken by his Word and I was going to obey Him: we would do anything to get our brother out of prison.

The release of Mossa, for whom the sun of justice rose on February 12, 2010, prompts me to never forget that it is God who always has the last word. *"But for you, who revere my name, the sun of righteousness will rise, with healing in its wings. And you will go out and leap like calves released from the stall."* (Malachi 4:2)

I now dream of a day when Afghanistan will practice human rights and all Afghan Christians will return home! They will then be bearers of the good news of God's salvation through Jesus Christ!

Part 6: The Uprooting

Chapter Thirty-Four

Dark Clouds

All was well under the 2013 Afghan sky. The work of the Pelican was growing and consolidating. For ten years now we had been serving the Hazaras, and we saw the progress made with real satisfaction, which amply rewarded our efforts. The Pelican, a symbol of Christ, was weighed down by an increasing number of pupils, and women, children, and the deaf who huddled under its wings.

On the other hand, since the closure of the café, the bakery apprenticeship program had slowed down. Our most important customer, the Atmosphere Restaurant, had drastically reduced its orders. Danger once again had pulled the rug out from under the feet of the boldest entrepreneurs. After various attacks in the neighborhood and a kidnapping attempt, the restaurant decided to close its doors a few months later. Fortunately, the French Embassy and some NGOs could not do without our croissants, and the pastries prepared by the Pelican still delighted participants at their meetings. So even if the apprentices were no longer as busy as they had been in the days of the café, they still enjoyed a good salary, hearty breakfasts, and almost father-son relationships with Jacques.

In Afghanistan, adaptability and perseverance are indispensable qualities for those desiring to remain in the country. The little store we had opened in town after the closure of the café became a good illustration of this. Not only did the bakery continue to operate, but the apprentices were now also trained in sales.

Jacques conducted this business as he did all his life's projects. Like a regular drumbeat, his entrepreneurial spirit and keen intelligence helped him find solutions once again when everything seemed blocked. Three high tables made it possible to have a cup of coffee, a cup of tea, or lunch on the go. This meeting place in the heart of Kabul took us back a few years: "We are redoing, in a very small way, our Croissanterie in France," joked Jacques with a complicit smile!

★★★

Mid-February 2013, at 4:00 a.m., Jacques returned from the bakery as usual, leaving the apprentices to finish up without him. He clutched a still-warm baguette for breakfast in his hand. It was the start of a day like any other. I served tea, and he read the Bible aloud, the routine of the Afghan dawn.

Later, entering our room to change, eyes clouded with tears, he stared at me intensely. His voice trembled with emotion—sadness and relief mingled strangely.

"Ariane, I know that I am forgiven. We're going to have to be very brave…especially you!"

I did not quite understand his words or his solemn tone. I believe today that the Spirit of God was warning him of his possible departure. He had to know, to be convinced, that whatever happened, it wouldn't be so serious. He had to understand that because he was forgiven, his future was assured, planned for all eternity. This child of the Most High, this disciple of Jesus had nothing to fear from the terrible storm that was coming. We had to stay calm. We had to remain confident. We had to keep our faith intact, in the face of future events.

Yet I still hear myself joking, "But Jacques, you've known for a long time that you've been forgiven. What's got into you today?"

His moist gaze and softly spoken words hurt me so much. "Yes, but today I know it differently. This truth imprinted itself in me, it invaded my heart and my entire being. I know that whatever happens to us, we are in His hand and nothing, therefore, can disturb our final destination."

I remained silent, paralyzed by his words, shocked by the severity of his gaze and his persuasive tone. He seemed to have access by premonition to a piece of his near future.

Jacques' faith in his Savior, this faith-passion which removed obstacles and made us bounce back after so many battles, this unshakable faith was to serve us in our distress from that morning on. It became our active companion for eight months.

A rehearsing of the events quickly made me realize that it had all started a week before Jacques' strange declaration. While we were having lunch with friends in a restaurant in Kabul, he felt the first signs of a terrible illness. The rice that day seemed to get stuck in his throat. With his healthy appetite, he had ordered one of the heartiest dishes on the menu. Not understanding what was happening to him, he left the table for a few moments and returned to finish his plate with apparent calm.

But a monstrous wave of anxiety washed over my heart and mind. I was scared. I relived the dread of the first signs of my little boy's illness. I remember that I had, in this restaurant, a physical manifestation of panic, which only those who have experienced this apprehension can understand: heart pounding, inability to swallow anything, trying despite everything, through casual conversation, to cling to the normality of life. I think today that in a way, I too had been warned by heaven.

This period was immensely agonizing. I watched Jacques swallow as he ate his meals. He was hungry and working normally, so I told myself that, tired and stressed with too much coffee, I had probably overdramatized the situation. Driven by his usual enthusiasm and energy, my super-husband treated this blockage of food with contempt, until the day when it no longer descended into his stomach while we had lunch with our Afghan teammates. Their glances revealed a worried curiosity. Although he never mentioned it to me to protect me, I felt he was unusually concerned. I dared not ask him anything, petrified by the idea of an alarming response.

At that time, the expatriate Christians of Kabul were preparing to celebrate Easter and Jacques very joyfully accepted the request by the British pastor that the "Pélican Boulanger" prepare the buffet for this ceremony.

Enchanted by the idea of delighting the international community with typical French foods, Jacques meticulously planned the preparation of the sumptuous buffet!

I worried more and more, and I finally talked to him about it, urging him to return to France for a proper medical examination. Finally, he agreed to contact my sister and explain his health problems to her. The next day Marie-Laure gave us the advice of the French doctors who had been informed. They all insisted on the urgency of our return to France. We left Afghanistan on March 25, 2013.

On the way to the airport, our Afghan administrator was worried to hear his boss and colleague, Jacques, announce to him with a touch of sadness, "You are now the head of the NGO in Afghanistan. I entrust the Pelican to you; if my health problem is not serious, we will be back next week. Otherwise…I'm counting on you!"

Again, I hated the tone he took at the end of this statement.

On the plane back to France, I could not help the pangs of anguish assailing me from all sides; mealtimes were a torment to me. In Dubai, half of the sandwich remained on his plate. I panicked. I couldn't bear the idea of the suffering that perhaps awaited us. I couldn't bear the idea of Jacques being sick. I could not bear to relive the hell of seeing the one I loved most in the world plunged into physical pain, as my son had been. My heart was imploding. I felt a terrifying commotion rock my insides. My whole body fought against what my mind could not accept.

Our impromptu arrival in Alsace was filled with emotion. Alas, Jacques was unable to swallow the veal blanquette so kindly prepared by the wife of the president of Le Pélican, once again proving a serious problem. But I was still clinging to a thread of hope. Since the first exams showed nothing abnormal, I wanted to remain confident. Jacques would be treated and cured quickly, and we would return to Afghanistan as soon as possible. After the hasty departure, this was my new plan, and I didn't want any other!

But just before Easter, the first few worrying diagnoses came one after another, like so many daggers piercing my heart. A large cancerous tumor blocked the bottom of Jacques' esophagus, also impacting half of his stomach. Then we learned that the cancer had already metastasized, invading his liver and right lung. We understood how serious it was and neither of us retreated into denial.

We knew perfectly well that death, without the miraculous intervention of the Lord, was looming on the horizon. Yet we kept our hearts anchored in faith and courage. We relied on certain promises of God, knowing that He was working wonders, even today. As was possible over 2,000 years ago, God could heal Jacques today.

His strength of character, his appetite for life, and his unfailing faith forced me not to crack. I continued to smile and fight against the disease with him. But this fight proved to be fierce against the violence of a cancer that had only declared itself when it was sure to win.

During Easter worship at our Mennonite church in Ingersheim, I pleaded with the Lord to heal the love of my life. I gave God the whole program of what we still had to accomplish and the method to undertake the healing of Jacques. I told Him about the project in Afghanistan that we both wanted to continue and grow. I reaffirmed to him our faith, which we relied upon to help us win against the malignant cells. I explained to him the chemo attacking the cancer, but also leaving Jacques panting and without any strength. I told him all this in detail with words chosen for him to understand... as if the Creator of the Universe did not know! As if the Lord of Life had taken his gaze away from us!

Then, finally, exhausted with sadness, I let go when the words of Jesus, without warning or any control on my part, took possession of my panicked heart. I know that I did not intellectually think this sentence, it came to me, sweet, pure, and haunting, straight from the heart of God. *"Not my will, but yours be done," (Luke 22:42)* said Jesus, addressing his Father in the Garden of Gethsemane.

These words of Jesus filled my heart and my soul, revealing the path of submission and total surrender. So, I took up the phrase of the Son as my own and, trembling, whispered it to the Father.

I will never take that thought back nor regret it. I still use it today. This is my way of being with the Lord, my logic, and my peace. If I admit once and for all that it is he who knows, that it is he who holds the world and every living being in his hand, if I have enough faith to live through the dramatic events, in the perspective of his promise of eternal life, then I must submit myself to him completely—my life and my future. I, therefore, admitted at that moment that I should perhaps also surrender Jacques to him, who was his and not mine.

The terrible battle against the disease began. It lasted eight months—eight months of conquests and battles, of hope and victories, but also of disappointment, anguish and blind panic. I knew this time that love was not always enough. Nor was I naïve enough to believe that God would necessarily heal Jacques. I believed him capable of it, but I also knew he was sovereign, and I admitted that his will might not agree with mine.

I was experiencing Jacques' cancer as I had experienced my little boy's--violently, energetically, bitterly, braced in the fight. The battle plan was organized: specialized hospitals, renowned oncologists, targeted chemotherapy treatments. The pawns took their places for a brutal fight, which, with our still intact optimism and our constant faith, we thought we would win.

In the fall of 2013, the doctors authorized us to go on vacation to southern France. This time of rest and sport had been planned long before the onset of the disease. From Kabul, Jacques had booked a golf vacation on one of the most beautiful European courses. "You will write the book (this one), and I will improve my golf. If you've done well and I've made progress on the course, we'll have a glass of champagne in the evening when I get back."

Since completing my first book *Hearts to Heart*, Jacques wanted me to write a second book to tell about the encounter that had changed our lives: our reconciliation with Jesus, the Nazarene.

I wrote nothing, not a line, not a word, not a comma during those few days away from the hospital. We had breakfast together, then Jacques joined his golf teacher. He came back exhausted, but happy with the

advice and new tricks the pro had taught him. Classes only took place
in the morning. So, after a short nap, we went back to the course where
Jacques tried to apply his teacher's advice. Having become his favorite
caddy, I tried to do my job well, pulling the cart at his pace to the next
hole!

During the lessons and on the course, Jacques earned the admiration
of his coach who was aware of his illness. Going well beyond reasonable
limits, he forgot his cancer and despite his fatigue, often shot rounds
with scores quite worthy of the very good player he was. The question
of whether there were golf courses in heaven seemed to preoccupy him.

Often, while he was looking for a lost ball in the undergrowth, I
would swallow back the tears that regularly filled my eyes. I had so much
trouble seeing him so thin and tiring so quickly. The contrast between my
confusion, the beauty of the site, and the charm of the hotel provoked in
me a bitter revolt.

The last dinner in this five-star hotel in Taulane gave me a glimpse of
the drama that would assail us a few days later. Jacques hardly ate anything
anymore and handed me his glass of champagne wearily. I was floored.
Anguish knotted my throat and an immeasurable sadness settled deep
inside me.

I remember that when we left, the receptionist asked us if we were happy
with the stay and if we were thinking of coming back the following year.
"Why not?" I murmured. Jacques said nothing, as he pretended to go
through the invoice.

For our return to Alsace, I took the wheel spontaneously whereas he
had driven on the way there. Without talking about it, we both sensed the
horrible feeling of being almost at the end of the road. Not commenting
on what was happening in his body, certainly to spare me, he still could
not hide the exhaustion that overwhelmed him. The knife, that stabbed
us at the time of the diagnosis, seemed to cut deeper. I felt it insidiously
making its mark in our hearts.

During our lunch break at a roadside rest stop, he suddenly got up
and ran to the bathroom. Leaving a note on the table, I immediately

left and joined him outside. We took a few steps and without a word, Jacques hugged me. Both of us were unable to express to each other the immense distress that had savagely overtaken us; we remained silent for a few moments, then throughout the rest of the journey.

The next day, at Strasbourg Hospital, the fatal diagnosis confirmed the total destruction of the meager hopes allowed by the previous medical results. The wet eyes of Jacques' doctor, this high-level oncologist, as well as his few words full of modest compassion, led us to understand that Jacques' life was taking its last turn.

We returned home for a few days of the intimate life we had left. This week, away from treatments, left me with a taste of honey and bitterness at the same time. Cradled by very sweet moments, filled with tenderness and love in which neither of us mentioned the future, we let life pass by unaware of anything else. For the first time in thirty-nine years together, we had no plans. We painfully felt that the hour of separation was coming. Each protected the other and avoided words that could hurt. The attitudes, the looks, the stolen kisses, and the modest words whispered in one breath were the last privileged moments of freedom to love each other that cancer had not yet stolen.

Then we knew it, there would be the return to the hospital and time would again be chopped up by care, meals, waiting for results, and anxiety. We would inevitably enter the process leading from life to death.

Chapter Thirty-Five

Broken Wings

S oon, the disease redoubled its grip and triumphantly launched its last offensive: Jacques entered the Colmar Hospital in an emergency and then was admitted to the Strasbourg Hospital. Visits and expressions of affection helped us to live each new day. I hoped, beyond reason and without really believing in it, for an extreme intervention on the part of the One who had created this body dying in front of me. Jacques, in a spiritual form beyond the ordinary, continued to radiate a passionate faith. He was often heard to say, "I don't care whether the Lord heals me or calls me, I know where I'm going." Then he added, turning to me: "But I am so sad to leave you, Ariane…"

Impossible to hear this sentence without crying, I turned my head away and gathering my feeble strength, I ordered my body to calm down and my heart to welcome the inevitable. Yet I was capsizing inside, caught up in abysmal despair. Jacques was leaving me, and I couldn't hold him back. Certain of his final destination, he was at peace and shared his faith all around!

The day before his death, we had a visit from a priest who, as he left, could not help saying, "Your faith, Jacques, is exemplary. I have never met anyone like you!" Full of compassion and the love of Christ, he walked out of the room completely overwhelmed and perhaps also exhilarated in his own faith. Indeed our testimony of the encounter with Christ, told by Jacques, whose enthusiastic passion had not weakened, had dazzled this man, making him even forget to propose the last sacraments, which are normally always done in such cases.

This priest, filled with the Holy Spirit, understood that the soul of Jacques, preparing to leave his body, had been accepted by God from all eternity. His salvation was guaranteed, there was nothing to add. No frills or embellishments… only the purity of the original faith and dialogue with the Father were in order.

Then everything went downhill very quickly. The next day would be our last day together.

On November 15th, in the morning, I realized that we were at the end. We were at the end of our story on earth, and of our life together. For me, that meant the end of it all. Jacques' path ended there, but mine unfortunately continued; our wish to die together was not granted.

So I spoke to Jacques and reaffirmed my love to him, reminding him that Jesus was there at the foot of the bed, that the room was full of angels, and that I was very close to him, with him. These were my last words, to which he could no longer respond. But having heard me, he smiled at me and gently squeezed my hand, as if to nod and perhaps assure me of his eternal love.

Did he already see what I was unable to see, entangled in such limited humanity? Jacques was preparing to leave for the beyond which awaits us and for which Jesus has opened the way. He took off, he, this retired parachutist with more than 4,000 jumps, but this time in the opposite direction! Up to the House of the Father, far from earthly tribulations, he would find the original freedom and enjoy the absolute happiness of finally contemplating the face of God and rediscovering the Father's smile at his son.

Late at night, I dozed off on that hospital bed, lulled by his breathing. Then suddenly, the deafening silence of the room woke me. No breath left the body of Jacques who, on tiptoe, had left without waking me, protecting me until the very last moment.

Like August 25, 1988, November 16, 2013, will never fade from my memory. The second stab, right next to that caused by the death of Frantz will remain a gaping wound until the day of our reunion on the other side.

Would my faith ease the pain of Jacques' absence and help me to keep on living?

I leaned over this emaciated body that had ceased to live. He was only sixty-six years old. I looked at his beautiful face, his eyes still looking at me. Very gently I closed his eyes and sobbed.

Quickly, fragments of our life surfaced in my memory and invaded my heart. Snuggled up against him, I remembered his brash character, his personality that I had loved so much. This passionate fighter, ready for any adventure, this man of subtle intelligence, courage, and relentless action, lay there in front of me, defeated and victorious at the same time. Cancer had taken over his body, but his soul, I knew, had received its inheritance: the victory of the Lord over death. Jacques had entered eternal life.

He had "fought the good fight" and kept the faith to his last breath. Sure to be welcomed as a good and faithful servant who would henceforth share the joy of his Master, he disappeared from this world peacefully.

His master replied, 'Well done, good and faithful servant! You have been faithful with a few things; I will put you in charge of many things. Come and share your master's happiness!" (Matthew 25:21)

An incredibly brutal, wrenching agony arose in me, because despite this death foretold, I felt an intolerable mutilation in my own body, and I immediately felt the pain of a missing limb. At the same time, I had the impression of detaching myself from the world, and of eclipsing myself in a certain way, while a void full of the presence of Jacques invaded me. I also understood the absence that I would now have to subdue and manage.

Glued to the body of Jacques, I waited for the first light of dawn to tell my family, Jacques' brother, and my closest friends.

Chapter Thirty-Six

The Goodbye

In this strangely frozen time, the door opened slowly and let in the night nurse wishing to bring me coffee and comfort. I couldn't tolerate her arms or her smoky breath, and, shaking my head, refused the black liquid and her cold ashtray kiss. I found any kind of outward gesture of tenderness odious since the very source of the one I had drunk from for thirty-nine years had dried up forever. This reluctance to accept other people's hugs or demonstrations of love has never diminished and I wear it in my heart like Jacques' wristwatch on my wrist.

The day was breaking in Strasbourg, the sun was rising, and life without him was beginning.

Still stretched out against him, I did not hear my sister, Marie-Laure, and her husband, Henri, come in, but suddenly I noticed their compassionate presence. The automaton that I was eventually broke away from Jacques and stammered that I had to gather his things. On the bedside table, the little blue book containing the Psalms and the Gospels was waiting for a hand that now did not move. I took it with emotion and immediately thought that it would prolong the spiritual conversations between Jacques and my cousin, Jacqueline, when I gave it to her from him, like a testimonial gift from a *madman of God* to this one who questioned him so often on his faith and who still questions him today through these Scriptures.

The hospital morgue quickly received the body that I did not want to see there again. As with Frantz, I had the bitter feeling of a rush of actions from which I could not escape: fleeing the room and reentering the world of the living by tending to a dead person who had to be gotten *rid of.* This unbearable discrepancy reached its climax at the Strasbourg funeral parlor. When we walked through the door, the *soothing* decor, the new-age music, the room's scent, and the multicolored bouquets shocked me violently with their show of evading death. This artificial and cloying atmosphere sought to camouflage the reality of mourning, and I felt great disgust.

Then an elegant man held out his hand, offered his condolences with a sorrowful expression, and invited us to sit down in his office. I believe Henri took the floor and explained the situation of his brother-in-law who had died in the night at the nearby hospital and the need to repatriate the body to Colmar. The man in black, pleased to have a client, suggested a whole range of luxurious coffins and offered to serve us coffee. So, as he walked away towards the machine, I jumped up and decided to leave immediately: "We're off, we're going to Colmar," I whispered to my sister and her husband.

Everyone was silent in the car as Henri slowly drove. Through the window, I looked without seeing the landscape passing by my indifferent eyes. In my dazed state, I heard Marie-Laure call Freddy Fritsch, the president of Le Pélican, because practical things don't wait: we needed a funeral home.

An hour later, we entered a new establishment opposite the Colmar Hospital where I found a very different welcome. The gaze of the man sitting in front of me reflected a sense of acceptance of human finitude, and in the dimness of the room, the ravaged faces were no longer incongruous. I also noticed the layout of the store in line with its activity and that gave me confidence. We had left the *masquerade* of Strasbourg and its artificial and sweet atmosphere because here everything modestly reminded us of the reason for our visit. So, regaining control, I explained what I wanted: Jacques would be cremated in Strasbourg and then the urn would go to the cemetery of Ingersheim where his son had preceded him.

An ecumenical ceremony was organized by his family in Biarritz on November 23, and I organized a memorial service in Alsace on November 29, in which I wanted to give glory to God and honor the memory of the one who had joined Him. During a sad evening with members of our church family, I chose the songs, and we organized the worship. Daniel, our faithful friend of fourteen years, had been publicly pointed out by Jacques in a church meeting: "I think the Lord is going to heal me, but if He doesn't, you are the one I appoint to preach at my funeral."

Then came the difficult question of the obituary to be written, a task that seemed me to be an insurmountable ordeal despite the insistence of the people preparing the service with me. My cousin Jacqueline, who had arrived the day before, agreed to help me and listened to me all night long with tenderness and compassion. This trip back in time through our memories brought us many tears but also smiles by reliving scenes where Jacques, the eternal joker, had made us laugh out loud. Jacqueline, who had also lost the love of her life, understood me without any words needed. We both knew that grief is impossible to share, unspeakable and permanent.

***

On Friday, November 29, 2013, the church of Ingersheim struggled to accommodate over three hundred people who had come to say a last farewell to Jacques Hiriart. They came from all over France but also from the USA, Switzerland, Germany, and Luxembourg. All kinds of people were gathered together that day: believers and non-believers, Protestants, Evangelicals, Catholics, Jews, and perhaps even Freemasons. Rotary members also came, from the club Jacques helped to found, golfers, the board members of the Pélican as well as many supporters and even a former instructor from our skydiving club. This heterogeneous mixture revealed the personality of Jacques whose authentic faith always commanded respect, even from people with very different beliefs.

The ceremony began with a warm welcome from Christian Sattler, president of the assembly, who knew how to find the right words to introduce Jacques and give an overview of the course of the service. After the reading of Psalm 40 and a song, Jacqueline recounted Jacques' life journey, "to better understand the rare man that he had been." She ended thus:

Looking back, we realize that there is a red thread, called the Holy Spirit, which protected and led this couple. Yes, the Lord was there. What now then?

Now it continues. The red thread is not cut. God is always there.

Ariane does not take up the torch: she keeps it. And she's going back to Afghanistan. Jacques will live on through the work of the Pélican. And Ariane will continue with the help of the friends of the Pélican to support and advance the project.

For the Love of God. For the Love of Afghans. And of course for the Love of Jacques.

After these intensely emotional words, the magnificent voice of our friend Paul Widmer rose with force in a moving German song. Then came the touching testimonies of Nancy, Paul, Jacky, and Laure, each wanting to pay a personal tribute to Jacques. Then Marie-Laure read a message from our Christian friend Mossa, for whom Jacques had fought so hard during his incarceration in Kabul. His admiration for him was boundless, and he reaffirmed his respect for the precious help of the Pélican, naming Jacques "the father and protector of thousands of Hazara children and women."

Freddy, the President of the Pélican took up the words of the Afghan administrator, who expressed the sorrow of having lost his boss and friend. Rachel from the Pélican board, took charge of reading the text from the United States, from Gladys, who remembered so well the good and bad times spent together in Afghanistan. In conclusion, she imagined that our two husbands, friends and accomplices who got to know each other in a choir in Kabul, were now singing, with happiness, at the feet of the Lord.

Overcome, I nevertheless headed for the platform to offer Jacques my testimony of love and renew my trust in God:

I had the pleasure of spending forty years of my life with Jacques. He was for me much more than a husband, he was my traveling companion, my accomplice, my support, my spare wheel, my alter ego, the best part of myself, the most solid and the most courageous.

He was a man of vision, fearless. Neither in Kabul, nor in the face of illness, nor at the gates of death, did he tremble. He knew where he was going, and he was going there with courage and confidence. Never did any compromise pollute his intellectual honesty or his spiritual commitment. His convictions were deeply anchored in the Word of God, this Bible, that he so loved to read and meditate upon.

Left alone by the side of the road, I don't know how I will finish the race, nor with what strength, nor with what determination. But I know the One who will be with me and carry me when I am unable to move on. Jesus Christ is the same yesterday, today and tomorrow. His grace will be sufficient each day to show me the path of the divine will.

So, despite the immense sorrow of no longer having him by my side, I choose not to be desperate.

"Thy will be done on earth as it is in heaven," this is not a trivial phrase that is said lightly…

"The Lord gave, the Lord took away, the name of the Lord be praised," said Job. I say it too!

Daniel preached according to Jacques' formal wish. He evoked their deep and fraternal friendship and urged me to continue on the path. Then Erwin Wild, vice-president of the Pélican, played a splendid flute solo to honor his affection for Jacques and me.

The church then seemed illuminated by the presence of Jesus, and I felt wrapped in Jacques' love…

Chapter Thirty-Seven

The Call

T he next day everyone had to leave except Bill and Nancy and my dear cousin Jacqueline who decided to stay a few more days to support me. I have practically forgotten everything about that time except their kindness, their prayers, and the few outings we took together…Jacqueline taking my arm when the four of us were walking in the streets of Colmar with its magnificent Christmas décor…the spicy mulled wine that turned our heads, while the coarse salt from the pretzels mingled with my tears…the bottle of champagne that we opened together to celebrate Jacques' entry into paradise…

Eventually, they would all return home, and the empty house resounded with deafening loneliness. The luminous being that Jacques had been, however, still shone after his passing, and those who loved him tried to bring me some warmth and consolation. At that time, I was sometimes surprised by anonymous hands leaving all kinds of small gifts at my door: flowers, cakes, books, and messages. Unable to meet anyone, I resumed the path of solitude, my great friend. Like a bird looking for a place to die, I curled up in my grief.

The nights filled with despair brought me painfully to dawn with the feeling that nothing more existed and that I would do well to disappear.

Despite everything, a survival instinct prompted me to accept the Newbranders' invitation to spend two weeks with them in Boston. Their affection, compassion and generosity found no words strong enough to express.

As a real sleepwalker, I took the train on the morning of December 25th after spending Christmas night in the hotel across from the station. In Boston, the wonderfully loving welcome of Nancy and her family delicately tended my open wound. And for two weeks my very dear friends cared with great compassion and love for the broken woman that I had become.

It was during this American stay that I received a sign from God. Sharon, Nancy's daughter, had a dream and she felt it was sent for me. She saw a cohort of tall men in flamboyantly white tunics encamped around the house. When she woke up, this nearly 40 year old lawyer, unaccustomed to spiritual dreams, nevertheless shared her dream with her mother. "I knew they were here because Ariane is here," Then she clearly expressed her certainty that the dream exemplified that God's special protection was granted to me by these angels in action.

On my return to France, still stimulated by the encouragement of my friend Nancy, I planned to go back to Afghanistan. However in my shattered mind revolved around one or two questions that remained unanswered for some time. What about me? Of my faith and my struggles? It would be difficult to live up to the example set by Jacques. Where would I find the will to continue my life without the one who helped me to stand up, without his reassuring presence, his enveloping tenderness, and his passionate love? How could I survive without one who borrowed the words of the Bible, to bring sweetness and hope to my ills, sealing the cracks in my soul? The one I loved above all else had gone on the path of eternity and I was left alone, with an incurable sorrow.

Unlike the spiritual void that was mine at the time of my child's death, I now understood that only the Spirit of the Risen One could escort me in my new existence. So I cried out to Jesus and trusted him. I offered him my tears like so many drops to be transformed into pearls of light, which he would bring to the Father as a sacrifice of adoration. I knew that Jacques, happier and more alive than ever, savored perfect joy. His peace and happiness were in no way comparable to earthly pleasures, even those experienced with me on the golf courses, his two passions!

But I was still oscillating between weariness, discouragement, and fear, and if I felt a strong desire to go back to Afghanistan, I still doubted my abilities. I knew very well the fragility of my situation and the enormous difficulty of coping with it. No sooner had I mentioned a future departure than a wave of anxiety with its share of physical symptoms fell mercilessly upon me, immediately sweeping away my desire. I heard almost audibly: "It's impossible, you're not going to make it!"

Around me, no one was deciding for me, only I could make the decision. Cut off from the church by my need for solitude and the morbid anguish of being around others, holed up at home in a daze, I had practically no contact with the outside world, rarely answering the phone. At that time there was for me only a single, vertical, and uninterrupted dialogue nourished by prayers and biblical readings. As in the days of our spiritual search, I needed God and nothing else!

Around three o'clock in the morning, like every night since Jacques' death, I went down to the kitchen and made tea. I heard the rain hitting the leaves of the trees in the garden, which, then swollen with water, drifted gently down to die on the gravel. I would have liked to be one of them and let the frost cover me then the cold numb me until the last sleep. The immutability of this scene, which is renewed each season, plunged me into an infinite nostalgia. From then on, I would watch nature die out and then be reborn alone without my companion. We would never again admire together the magnificence of God's creation on this earth.

Once again, my tears flowed abundantly and an immeasurable sadness invaded me until I fell asleep on the sofa in the living room, lulled by the wind in the branches of the hundred-year-old chestnut trees.

One day when I had slept a lot, surprised to see the late hour, I wanted to talk to my Father and follow the spiritual impulse that was guiding me. Immediately collapsing on the tiles, on my knees, my head buried in the sofa, I prayed and listened to the Master of the world and of my destiny. A few moments later a kind of injunction pushed me to finally go to the church where I had not returned since the memorial service. I only had ten minutes left to arrive on time for worship.

Parking the car as far as possible from the entrance to the church, totally terrified at the idea of facing the world, I waited, hidden behind the sun visor, for the last stragglers to disappear inside. Then I went up to the balcony to be there alone.

The preacher's message centered on the reality of a God who does his will through people who initially seem weak. *"Go in the strength you have...."* Gideon heard from God (Judges 6:14). And the anonymous young man became the valiant leader of a people in bondage, and the conqueror of the Midianites.

Immediately, this biblical account transformed my overwhelmed and indecisive state. I took over the sentence said to Gideon and I became "Private Geiger," thus finding my maiden name and that of my brave father: I would go to Afghanistan, with the strength of God. My decision that day was final.

Part Seven: The Transcendence

Chapter Thirty-Eight

Nevertheless

M y return to Kabul depended on administrative papers that were difficult to obtain. I had to formalize my status as the sole heir to obtain Jacques' bakery license since I also wanted to resume his vocational training work. During this extremely tense period, I felt the accompaniment of God at every turn.

At the worst moments of discouragement, winks from Heaven would arise, and the iconic Bible phrase, *"Trust in the Lord with all your heart" (Proverbs 3:5)*, would often invigorate me. We had discovered the wisdom of this verse twenty-five years earlier in Bible school. Now I had to apply it without moderation!

I thought of this advice at the Embassy of Afghanistan in Paris where among the visa applicants, I was waiting in a leaden atmosphere. After a few minutes, I walked into the office.

The man looked at my papers, then exclaimed in unfriendly English, "You came for nothing, no visas are issued anymore. It's Mr. Karzai's election and no one is allowed to enter Afghanistan."

Just a few minutes earlier an AFP (Agence France-Presse) journalist had warned me, "No chance, no visa at the moment!" I replied politely anyway, "I have to go back to Kabul. The apprentices from my husband's business are waiting for me, I have brought you the bakery license and all the necessary certificates translated into Pashtu. Everything is perfectly in order, you can check…if you please!"

The dark-eyed man scratched his mustache and I heard his secretary speaking in Dari, "She has everything she needs, her documents are in order."

Finally condescending to actually look at my papers, he said, "I told you that no visas are currently allowed, but...I'll make an exception for you. I take that responsibility on myself. You will have a one-month visa, don't ask for more and you will see it on the spot. Hurry up and pay the price of your visa at the post office, we do not accept checks, credit cards, or cash."

"You only have an hour left," added his secretary. "We close at half past twelve."

I had come from Colmar that very morning and had no intention of sleeping at a hotel. So I rushed to the post office they had mentioned, but it was not open. Then I ran to another post office, but when at last I reached the counter, I heard with horror that it was time for their break. Like a madwoman, I sped off to another neighborhood where I found a friendly employee who kindly advised me, "But ma'am, don't run like that! It's not healthy!" Finally catching my breath, I paid the price of the visa and hurried back to the embassy... which I reached just before closing time! After having informed my relatives of the unexpected success of my approach, I took advantage of the streets of Paris, so beautiful under the late winter sun, and strolled around feeling immense relief.

A few hours later, sitting on the TGV, a high-speed train, taking me back to Alsace, I thanked God for opening a door and also meditated on the Afghan proverb: "Harakat o Barakat": "It is in movement that we find the grace of God." This Paris marathon was proof of that!

Afghanistan was looming, and after four months of administrative battles, visa and plane ticket finally in hand, I began a new life in Afghanistan, but this time without the man of my life. I wanted, however, to give him his full place in my heart and my thoughts, despite his physical absence.

I dared not think of the new complications that my status as a widow would cause. Seasoned by Jacques, who always rushed in exclaiming,

"Let's go, Ariane! If it is God's will, no obstacle will stop us because he will fix them all!" I decided to imitate him.

Sitting near the window, I watched the sunrise as the plane flew over the first mountains of Afghanistan. I couldn't help but think of Jacques and his battle with illness. We had both hoped to return to Kabul. Memories of those eight months assailed my mind, sucking me into a sadness that I refused to reveal because I had to show courage and strength to the Afghans, and to myself. At that moment the passage from the New Testament that Jacques knew by heart and quoted while taking his doses of chemo came back to me, reminding me of the promises of eternity:

Therefore we do not lose heart. Though outwardly we are wasting away, yet inwardly we are being renewed day by day. For our light and momentary troubles are achieving for us an eternal glory that far outweighs them all. So we fix our eyes not on what is seen, but on what is unseen. For what is seen is temporary, but what is unseen is eternal." (2 Corinthians 4:16-18)

He would often say to me, emphasizing the words "an eternal glory that far outweighs them all." "But do you realize what that means Ariane? Do you realize what awaits us up there? It will be far beyond anything imaginable, beyond beauty, beyond description with our bland human words. It will be fantastic, it will be awe-inspiring!"

Then he added, taking my hand, "You must know these verses by heart, and never forget that we are made to join this glorious life with God. Keep them preciously in your heart. We need them…" I was silent. His look said: "You will need them."

I remembered all this as the plane landed hard on the tarmac. I immediately rediscovered the stress of the checks by the immigration and police officers, who still looked just as forbidding. My stomach twisted in anguish as I filled out the questionnaires. For the Afghans, I represented what they hate the most. A foreign woman with the worst flaw: no husband. In Islamic culture, I no longer existed. Without the protection of Jacques, I would now have to continue the fight only with the help of God. I made this observation that was both sad and, despite everything, promising because if I no longer had Jacques, I knew, on the other hand, that I could count on the presence of Jesus. Leaning in faith on the promise he had made to his disciples, just before leaving the earth, I gratefully welcomed a new courage which slowly settled in me:

"I have told you these things, so that in me you may have peace. In this world you will have trouble. But take heart! I have overcome the world." (John 16:33)

"And surely I am with you always, to the very end of the age." (Matthew 28:20)

After an hour drive, I entered the school.

In the courtyard, holding back tears and stammering their respectful affection, the guards articulated with difficulty their condolences. I think that without the restrictions of Afghan culture, they would have hugged me, and no doubt I would have been stuck there for a while.

On the other hand, the children, so accustomed to death and separation, did not express much. The cleaning women were the ones who showed their compassion the most: crying profusely, they crushed me against their chests. Some, widows for a long time, understood the difficulties related to my new status. The teachers had a hard time finding their words. Some, very close to me, unable to express their pain, simply wrapped their arms around me and sobbed. I shook many hands and kissed many wet cheeks on March 25, 2014, the day I returned after a year's absence.

Then in the evening, finally alone, I collapsed. I finally had the right to rest.

Later Barfie, my cat, very happy to have found me, jumped on the bed and fell asleep against my arm. *And now, what shall I do?* The line from Gilbert Bécaud's song sprang through the mists of my drowsiness, and I began to question heaven. Then three thoughts imposed themselves on me in such a clear way that a great calm came over me:

The Lord had chosen not to heal Jacques: I would choose to trust him.

The Lord had chosen to send me back to Afghanistan: I would choose to obey him.

I wanted to stay under the wings of the Most High and be in his plan. Maybe I would even find peace and a little rest there later.

Chapter Thirty-Nine

Flowers Among the Bushes

T he next day I tackled the problem of transferring the license of the bakery to my name. I no longer had time to cry. We had to act.

As in France, during my administrative negotiations, I experienced day after day the hand of God blessing my dealings with the Afghan government, one of the most corrupt on the planet. Each obstacle represented an insurmountable wall, which I managed to overcome despite everything. After four months of daily struggles, I finally obtained the transfer of the license giving me a six-month visa and authorization to resume the activities of the bakery. I heard, amused, the reflections of the expatriates:

"But Ariane, it usually takes a year and more if all goes well. How did you do it?"

So, looking up at the sky, my response rang out, mischievous and complicit, "I have someone powerful up there, and He wants me here!"

Without a doubt, it was a victory from the Lord.

These tough battles often dragged me into total discouragement during which times the negative little phrase, heard so many times in France, popped up incessantly in my weary mind: "What's the use?"

Yet another angel, Christine Medan, provided extraordinary support. A retired nurse, she had joined the Pelican project in Kabul at the beginning of Jacques' illness.

During the harsh time of my return to Afghanistan and the hour of my free fall into despair, this kind friend took me to her heart and prayed to the Lord for me. I will always be extremely grateful to her. Her jokes followed by shrill laughter sparked a burst of joy in me, and she also knew how to become serious again and console me. We read the Bible every morning and I found she had a talent for explaining it to me. She seemed to be more spiritual than I was. Jokingly, I gave her the nickname "little pocket pastor." She did a lot of good around her and when she left Afghanistan to bring the love of Jesus to other difficult countries, we all missed her.

The new Pelican school that Christine and I had established in Bamiyan, during and despite Jacques' illness, needed checking and I left for the Hazarajat as soon as possible. During the flight, I thought about the heartbreaking separation and wondered sadly about what I had believed to have been necessary. I was remembering those three weeks during which I had left Jacques sick in France. Now that he was dead, came the painful remorse for having sacrificed to the Pelican this little time of life with him.

However, we had made the decision together because we did not want to send Christine, the volunteer from Paris, alone. I had accompanied her to Afghanistan for the time necessary to create a school in Bamiyan, as we had planned before the illness.

***

Arriving at the hill of Sang e Chasspan, located on one of the plateaus on a cliff above Bamiyan, I had the impression of having found the place where the Pelican was to land. The destitution of the inhabitants of the region revolted me because neither water, nor electricity, nor trade, and, of course, no school served this population who were abandoned to their fate.

Along the road going up to the village, I observed that many of the old caves of monks from the Buddhist era had become dwelling places. Families with many children crowded inside them. These primitive dwellings without any comfort broke my heart, and I thought of the great Buddhas, whose shadows seemed to cry too.

Convinced that I had been guided, I immediately signed a rental contract to set up a school there.

Christine finished her mission in the summer of 2014 and in September, thanks to the inexhaustible providence of God, an English couple, Andrew and Sheila, joined me in Kabul, bringing me their life experience, their energy, and their affection. I could pray and share my worries with other Christians. They also relieved me of a lot of work. The expansion of our organization meant it was impossible for one person to do all the work. Their arrival at the Pelican was one more gift from heaven above!

When I look back, I realize that my path was paved with stepping-stones that always took me further. Because my path was watered with divine showers, extravagant flowers grew there amid bushes and precipices. The protection, inspiration, and grace of God were the essential ingredients in the development of this continuously embellished bouquet.

Chapter Forty

Seventy Times Seven Times

Perched on the cliffs of Bamiyan, the Pelican school quickly acquired a good reputation, and children flocked there from near and far. However, in August 2015, everything seemed to collapse when one night my window pane shattered under the impact of two large stones thrown from a slope on the hill. Terrified, I feverishly made tea that my guard and I drank in the yard.

Around four o'clock in the morning, the sun nonchalantly extricating itself from the cottony peaks, made me admire a most beautiful sunrise with its majesty over the mountain range of the Himalayas. As its rays darted over the sunflowers in the garden, I watched in amazement as a transcendent light burst forth illuminating everything in its path. Then, connected to heaven by a few invisible threads, I perceived even more the reality of the spiritual world, communicating to me a supernatural peace.

The police inspector immediately thought it was the revenge of a dismissed or disgruntled employee, a common reaction in this country. Hastily consulted, the village chiefs, pulling on their gray beards while sipping sweet tea, assured us that the population in no way wanted the NGO to leave. We were lost in guesswork because the unclaimed attack left a feeling of shame hanging over the whole village, that felt responsible.

The following days passed normally, and the anguish which had been rising in me at the onset of darkness since the attack gradually diminished. Installing big bars on my windows and having a second guard on the roof at night helped me regain my confidence. The life of the NGO continued its course and we forgot the incident, which we assumed had been the work of a bad kid acting out.

But at dawn on the following Sunday, I discovered a death threat on my cell phone: "Don't think the bars on your window will protect you! That was just a warning...It would be very easy for me to kill you."

The fact that this message also mentioned my English colleague, as well as other details of our work, indicated the closeness of its author. So the police officer had been right, we had an enemy on the inside who would probably not stop his attack.

Although in an extreme panic upon reading the message, I remembered someone who could help me. One of the pilots of an American airline transporting humanitarian workers lived in Bamiyan. He had given me his telephone number a few days earlier, in case I needed help. I called him immediately.

Understanding the real danger I was facing, he immediately invited me to take shelter in their guest house. A few moments later, the couple and their children welcomed me with open arms and offered me a bed, a shower, a delicious dinner, and above all wonderful comfort.

But I felt trapped because I could not stay in Bamiyan and above all did not want to endanger the lives of my hosts. I had to leave quickly. But repair work at the airstrip forced the airport to prohibit all flights until the end of the month, and it was only August 9th!

The Bamiyan-Kabul road, forbidden to foreigners by embassies, was regularly attacked by the Taliban who robbed, kidnapped, and killed travelers venturing on it. Despite the danger, I was forced to consider this possibility. I had to choose between two risks: staying in Bamiyan or trying to return to Kabul by the infamous road. Preferring action, I planned, along with the Afghan head of the school, my escape by car. The next day, well before dawn, hidden under a burka, like a blue ghost, I dashed into the Pelican's 4x4 in which my Afghan colleagues were waiting for me, along with their wives and babies. We had come up with this subterfuge to go as unnoticed as possible and make it look like a trip by an Afghan family.

After we got through the first two checkpoints without any problem, the road opened up in front of us, arid and threatening. I was suffocating under my burka. While I caught glimpses of a lunar landscape through the blue mesh, I thought of my friends who had died on Afghan soil. Would it be my turn soon? The "run for your life" feeling on this road, was it only a lack of courage or was it a warning of my next destination in the afterlife? I couldn't hold back my tears when the memories of those familiar faces came flooding into my mind, and I missed Jacques' presence unbearably. What was I doing on this road in the middle of nowhere? And what was I pursuing in this dangerous country?

Approaching *Pashtun land*, the most dangerous portion of the journey, since it is inhabited by the Pashtun ethnic group from which the Taliban come, a heavy silence of anguish stagnated in the car, when, instinctively warned, even the babies were silent.

Seven long hours passed before reaching the suburbs of the Afghan capital. The danger averted, the toddlers began to scream again, the mothers, to chat pleasantly, and the driver, finally relaxed, hummed an Afghan tune. The suspended time of crossing the enemy terrain was forgotten in a sigh; life returned to normal, and I finally could take off my burka!

The French embassy informed the highest authorities of the Afghan police of the attack and threats made against me. They commenced an investigation, and ten days later, we knew the one who had committed these aggressions: the supervisor of the school of Bamiyan! He had a charming smile, but he had nevertheless not respected Pelican ethics. By lecturing him, I had wounded the pride of a Muslim man who could no longer bear to be ruled by a woman, and an infidel no less! The violence of his actions revealed the depth of his humiliation, and I now measured the consequences of my lack of tact.

Sadly, we suspended the activities of the Bamiyan school.

Two months passed before our return to that city. While my Afghan administrator encouraged me to definitively close this project, my English team members, connected to heaven, retorted, "We must wait and pray."

But since I felt responsible for the safety of my colleagues, I hastily decided to close the school and announce it to the village elders. During the night, dissatisfied with my choice, I couldn't sleep. In the early morning, I opened my Bible to the page indicated by the Christian calendar and there I read, "*Then Peter came to Jesus and asked, 'Lord, how many times shall I forgive my brother when he sins against me? Up to seven times?' Jesus answered, 'I tell you, not seven times, but seventy times seven times.'*" (Matthew 18:21,22)

I received at that moment God's essential message: it was necessary to forgive infinitely, and I had to obey Him. I could almost hear the angels sigh in relief.

On the day of the reopening, the children of the caves, those of the village, and the women came back to school with joyful enthusiasm. The schoolchildren, laughing, and eyes shining with satisfaction, entered the courtyard as proud conquerors of a space finally regained!

The women, more modest, expressed to me, with affectionate embraces, their pleasure at returning to the center to continue their education, but also to share a precious bond between neighbors and friends. The freedom they enjoyed at the center balanced their monotonous lives and had been missed immensely during the two months of closure. I once again had proof of the worth of our program.

That day, I savored an unparalleled joy and was thrilled with the calm of my heart that had been so tormented until then. I recognized the peace of which Jesus speaks, that which passes all understanding.

Life on the hill resumed its course, and I noticed a redoubled friendliness on the part of the families who, running into me in the street, asked me about my health, my family, if I was too hot or too cold, or if I was inconvenienced by the recent sandstorm.

My English colleagues had returned to Kabul. So I remained alone in Bamiyan, going back to my office and reorganizing the functioning of the school: the repentant supervisor would be helped by a second young man, and would no longer have all the power. This pairing would prove to be very effective for the education program and for the teachers.

Moreover, this exemplary collaboration would push the community towards a mechanism of peace that had been overlooked until then. These young colleagues came from opposing enemy clans, and their fathers were the leaders. The two ethnic groups had hated and fought each other for generations. Bringing these boys together in common work for the benefit of the whole community represented a challenge but also a way to finally enter into a peace process.

These last events gave me much to ponder, and I meditated more deeply on my faith and my Christian commitment. I realized that resuming activities at the Bamiyan Center stemmed from my obedience to Jesus. This case not only benefited the Afghans; it also enlightened me and helped me further understand Jesus' response to Peter.

I thought about the sacrifice of Jesus so that I would be forgiven by God and so that I would, in turn, forgive. As the dawn had chased the darkness from the room, light had entered my heart and I had made the choice to follow him, the tortured and dying God-man on a simple cross outside of Jerusalem who said: "*Father, forgive them for they know not what they do.*" These words would become the greatest proof of love the world had ever heard. Remembering all this, the irrepressible need to forgive and to oppose hate with love had transcended all other feelings. By reconciling myself with my offender, I was also reconciling with my soul.

Chapter Forty-One

Dr. Jekyll

In the spring of 2015, Sheila introduced me to Youssef, her former colleague at the International School in Kabul.

During the job interview, pleasantly surprised to see how well he spoke English, I thought that his experience at the American school would help to improve the teaching skills of our teachers. Moreover, his reputation as a Christian further inspired an unusual benevolence: I hired him on the spot.

At the end of his trial period, we proposed that he strengthen the project team in Bamiyan, which he gladly accepted. But during one of my stays there at the end of October, I observed some of his behaviors that did not correspond at all to the values of the Pelican, and certainly not to those of the Gospel.

This careful monitoring for several weeks allowed me to note many incidents, and I especially noticed his arrogant and discriminatory attitude toward two teachers of different ethnicities: one Tajik, and therefore Sunni, and the other an Hazara of Shiite faith.

But the most serious problem revealed itself during a sharp altercation with the Afghan administrator who also came from a different ethnicity. This serious lack of respect for his superior, dictated by a violently racist nature, revealed his true personality and I could not let such injustice rage at the Pelican. I decided to act quickly, but I wanted to wait for Andrew and Sheila to return from vacation in the next few days.

Upon his return, Andrew arranged an interview with the unpleasant employee. That day, Youssef arrived tense and aggressive, barely concealing his anger when he heard our grievances. His nervousness increased when, at the end of the discussion, Andrew suggested in a calm voice that we should find a solution to solve the problem together and start again on the right foot. Then leaping up from his chair, he barked shrilly, "I know how I'm going to solve the problem!"

Plunging his hand into his jacket pocket, he pulled out a large-caliber pistol, cocked it, and aimed it at my colleague's stomach. With British understatement, Andrew advised, "Youssef, I don't think it would be a good thing for you to do that."

Immediately the armed man turned to me and pointed the revolver right between my eyes. My heart racing, I thought I was about to die and despite everything, a crazy idea went through my head: *I hope he won't miss and tear off half of my face… I would be horrible the rest of my life!* Then without even realizing I was speaking, like in a nightmare I heard myself say in a weak voice, "Youssef, I have never disrespected you."

I had the intuition during this meeting that his pride had never consented to being under the orders of an administrator from another ethnic group, nor had he accepted the authority of a simple woman. This was just like the supervisor in Bamyan.

After a few seconds, Youssef turned around and fled, leaving us amazed to still be alive. I addressed my gratitude to the angels who, I thought, had kindly pushed him out.

Why is it hard to believe that angels are still active today, when they are mentioned so often in the Bible? Is it too wonderful or too unreal? In any case, let them be thanked here, for their obedience to the Lord and their benevolent actions toward human beings.

During the nights that followed, I often saw in my dreams the hideous grin of this man letting his hatred explode for no reason. I couldn't understand it because this time I hadn't made any mistakes and nothing in my behavior could have offended him. On the contrary, I had pampered him as a fellow Christian believer.

The day after the assault, a first attempt at reconciliation in a neutral location organized by Tom, an American pastor friend, ended in dismal failure. Because, at the end of the stormy conversation and despite Andrew and Tom's attempts at reconciliation, they could reach no amicable resolution. Youssef only shouted louder, and furiously throwing the money and his last salary slips in the faces of the expatriates, he abruptly fled.

We no longer knew what to do, and we needed the Light from Above more than ever. Only a helping hand from heaven would get us out of this, our human means and our intelligence had not been sufficient. So, utterly helpless, Andrew, Sheila, and I knelt in prayer, imploring God's help, and asking for his Grace and Spirit to guide us.

Again, the good hand of the Lord helped us. Indeed, how else could I explain the unexpected arrival of a mediator who was ready to negotiate a reconciliation with our enemy and his family?

During the journey leading us to Youssef's house, I prayed to God to help us, because the future of the NGO and perhaps that of our lives depended on this meeting's outcome.

We arrived in force: Andrew, Sheila, Saber, our Afghan administrator, the mediator, and I. We filed into the family's living room. Surrounded by the men of the family and a few neighbors, the father of our aggressor, a warlord known for his violence and his fights, gave us a chilly reception. We were rudely asked to sit on the toshaks (floor cushions) and were not offered the traditional tea or the customary greeting, "Salaam," in the purest tradition of the country. A banal conversation far from what concerned us all lasted at least half an hour, then died away into a heavy silence, animated only by furtive glances. Then Andrew, with a nod of his head, asked the mediator to open the discussion for which we had come.

Sitting next to his father, Youssef stared down at the carpet without looking up, his stony expression not a good sign. Then the "warlord" spoke in a voice as icy as it was contemptuous of the misdeeds for which the foreigners bore responsibility.

"You *kharegis* (foreigners) stay a few years in our country and then you leave, leaving behind problems arising from your mistakes due to your stupid ignorance of Afghanistan. You do not know the culture or the traditions. You do not respect the local rules. Then, forgetting that it is your fault, you are surprised to have troubles which sometimes end tragically."

These reproaches uttered aggressively by the turbaned, bearded man exasperated me by their unfairness and their arrogance. Faced with this severe and final judgment, the men slavishly nodded and were silent: the harshness of the tone contemptuously condemned us all.

Despite the ball of anguish squeezing my throat, a feeling of enormous rebellion took hold of me and compelled me to raise my hand and ask for the floor. Men, unaccustomed to this gesture from a woman, regarded me with amazement, but the warlord, very surprised at my knowledge of the Dari language and my audacity, with a broad and generous gesture, granted me permission to speak.

Inspired by the Holy Spirit and following the example of Jacques who did not let himself be told what to do, in a seemingly confident voice, I began:

"You should know that we arrived in Kabul in February 2000 during the Taliban era. And we have seen the injustices and discrimination against your Hazara people. That is why we decided to help you. Look, I'll show you where our first school was: right at the end of your street! It was in 2003! And you know, I've been living in your country for sixteen years and I know your culture. So don't confuse me with some foreigners, who, as you rightly said, only stay a short time and make mistakes. You should know that I love Afghanistan. The best way to help you is to educate your youth, and you know that too."

To their wide eyes and conciliatory expressions, I added:

"I have dedicated myself to the establishment of schools in your community and plan to stay a long time. Please consider what I have said."

The warlord cleared his throat. We were all hanging on his words because the verdict depended on him alone. His piercing eyes rested on me for a moment, then tugging on his beard, he said:

"I listened to you carefully. Here is how we solve a problem like this."

He gestured to put a big stone on our papers that explained the grievance, as is the custom for Afghans do when they make peace. Against

all expectations, my speech had borne fruit and had discredited
Youssef, because, like a perfect hypocrite, he had never informed his
father of my Afghan past or the important help provided by the Pelican
to his people. A different situation loomed now: the good guys and the
bad guys had abruptly changed sides.

On this twist, pulled off at the last minute, we signed an agreement
that definitively closed the deal. Then, having thanked our hosts, with
great relief, we quickly descended the stairs two hours after we had
arrived!

Out in the street, the would-be shooter caught up with us and slyly
asked us to forgive him. His request seemed insincere to me. It seemed
his motives were to not to be excluded from the circle of expatriates
providing visas, work, and money. In any case, I had already granted
him the forgiveness he requested in my heart and told him so.

I also noted that he offered no apologies to our Afghan colleague
whom he had shown unparalleled hatred and contempt. It was difficult
to believe in an authentic change of heart under these circumstances.
I put it rather in the dark category of opportunism.

On our drive back, during which time everyone was silent, I remembered the hero of Robert Louis Stevenson's book, "Dr. Jekyll and Mr.
Hyde." In that book, a man with a double personality. Dr. Jekyll, a kind
medical practitioner from a London district, transformed himself at
night into a horrible killer represented by Mr. Hyde. Like him, Youssef
had pretended to be someone else and had lied to us by concealing his
devious character for almost a year. I was angry with myself for not
having unmasked him before because he had no place at the Pelican.
But I believed I should use every bad experience as an opportunity to
grow spiritually. The lower I fell, the more I bounced back, growing
even closer to the Rabbi of Nazareth, whose conditions and principles
of love I had accepted. I forced myself to show great tolerance towards
the dishonest employee and continued on my way.

Just as we had every year since the beginning of the Pelican's presence
in Afghanistan, we celebrated Christmas. The games, the music, the skits,

the songs and the delicious Afghan meal washed down with Coca-Cola delighted the students and the staff.

When we arrived in the Hazara neighborhood in 2003, Jacques and I had decided never to deny our Christian identity, despite the danger that this could pose. Evangelizing in the manner of the missionaries, with biblical teaching given to the local population, was out of the question, but on the other hand, we would never stop explaining our faith to anyone interested. The Christmas celebration allowed us to share a little about Jesus, so once a year we took the opportunity to set the record straight concerning what is spoken of him in the Muslim world. These words provoked many questions among the team and the students. We often prolonged the conversations that started at Christmas and then allowed the Holy Spirit, certainly more effective than we, to act.

Despite Jacques' departure, I didn't change anything about the Pelican's way of doing things, and I continued to celebrate alone, among the Afghans, the arrival of the Messiah. When I took the floor to welcome the guests, I suddenly had a vision that angels fluttering here and there, straightening a poster, adjusting a garland, and breathing the joyful spirit of Christmas into each heart. In this surreal atmosphere, lost in my thoughts, I missed the two loves of my life, Frantz, who loved parties so much, and Jacques, who was so enthusiastic about telling the story of Jesus. But somehow a very sweet feeling came over me and I no longer felt abandoned. I felt like the invisible world was surrounding me and dozens of seraphim were cheering me on. This exceptional gift from my Father lifted a very small corner of the veil that day. Then, like the shepherds enlightened by the angels in the countryside of Bethlehem, a heavenly joy washed through me and absence became presence.

Laughter, like the multicolored balloons hanging everywhere, burst out loudly in the four corners of the school. At the end of the afternoon, as snow was falling, the children, giddy from so many games, pranks and joy, left with wide eyes filled with stars. And this contagious joy filled my heart with immense gratitude to God who had transformed my burden into the peaceful certainty of being on the right path.

Once again, He had blessed our school, and I recognized his hand, his divine protection, and the influence of his Spirit. Hearing again the echo of my laughter, mingled with that of young and old, I could not deny the return of a part of my joy. For me, it was undoubtedly the manifestation of the miracle of Christmas, where everything was now possible thanks to the Savior of the world's arrival on earth.

In the school, strewn with confetti and *Merry Christmas* streamers, I replayed in my mind all the events of that day and thought that everything had been perfect.

Chapter Forty-Two

Quicksand

T he guards, warned to refuse entry to the school to the would-be shooter, now checked visitors' identities through the mesh rectangle added to the gate. We were all trying to move on, but the sudden appearance of his malevolent face in my dreams woke me up in the middle of the night, leaving me feeling anxious for long hours. I then saw the imaginary stone that the father had placed on the deeds of the son, and I prayed that it would stay there. Over the weeks, however, consumed by my work, I gradually forgot my apprehension. The Pelican's life went back to normal, and we never heard from the furious administrator again!

The laughter and smiles of children, their success in school, the women's literacy classes, the joyous din of meals followed by brushing of teeth, the screams of joy during games and sports, the exuberance of the deaf students learning sign language, the hugs, the pranks and, and, the joyous atmosphere of the Pelican became Afghan gifts to me and encouraged me to get more and more involved. For many years, shared affection, mutual respect, and acceptance of our differences had forged links with the Hazara population that nothing could break.

So I vowed I would never allow myself to be discouraged by disappointments, betrayals, or even dangers, and that I would not give up hope in this country. I was embarking on my nineteenth year in Afghanistan, quite a slice of life! And I had learned a long time ago to put my will at the service of my faith because I know the One in whom I place all my trust. This is the reason why I walk serenely under the gaze of my Father, who, at the crossroads, said to me: "*This is the way, walk in it!*" (Isaiah 30:21).

The love deposited in my heart for this people is tinged with a taste of eternity because it comes from God who is its source and provider. This fiery feeling laughs at obstacles, not bending before fear. He engages in life that he then stimulates and transforms. Springing from the heart of the Father, it lodges in human hearts according to goodwill. I would like to continue to be this receptacle of God's passion for humanity for as long as possible. Through the Pelican, I want to push back ever further the limits of ignorance, injustice and poverty.

This little flame, entrusted to us in February 2000, blazes fiercely because no one extinguishes a fire lit by God himself. Over the years, this flame, which has become a passion, bursts out every day in a huge bonfire, lighting up the darkest corners of Afghanistan. And because it comes to me from God, this joy will henceforth be my strength: *"Do not grieve, for the joy of the Lord is your strength"* (Nehemiah 8:10).

★★★

Two years after "the adventure with the man with the gun," another Afghan story abruptly interrupted my moral tranquility and the work of the Pelican. I had gone to the United States to give a series of conferences organized by Nancy and her team. After two months in America, I landed in Kabul at the end of June 2017 and found my neighborhood, "Dasht e Barchi," as dusty as ever, teeming with colorful crowds.

All along the road through the neighborhood, I observed this world so different from the clean, beautiful, and organized country I had just left. Here chaos reigned everywhere, yet I felt at ease in this environment and the feeling of returning home came over me. I looked for the reasons for my attachment to these Hazaras, and I understood that in their poverty and their ignorance, they still appeared to me as the noble descendants of Genghis Khan, the proud conqueror of Central Asia. Near the school, people greeted me with a smile and a "Khosh amedé" (*Welcome with joy*) to which I replied "Khosh Baché." (*Be happy*) Then I heard, "Manda na baché et safar et khoub bud?" (*Don't be tired. Was your journey good?*) and other sentences I still hear from the families of the students of the

Pelican. In this country, polite interactions stem from ancestral traditions and are never forgotten, whatever the circumstances. They reveal the intrinsic friendliness and the never-failing welcome of the Afghans. They are the charm of a population that keeps smiling and retains its kindness despite their country being at war. Moved to hear my name shouted by the street children, I finally entered the school after the hour-and-a-half long journey from the airport, and was happily reunited with the staff, the students, and my cat!

I did not hold back the good news of the success of the fundraising in the United States, and I shared my desire to use this money to create a center dedicated to the sensory impaired. Every week, for lack of space, we had to turn away children and teenagers, and this was becoming more and more unbearable to me. We were already dealing with deaf children, but a passionate ardor pushed me to widen the circle of these hearing impaired students and improve their program. A meeting with Rita, the sign language education manager, and Nasima, my coordinator, confirmed that my idea was the right choice because it met a critical need of the population.

One day, Saber, the project administrator, asked me for a few days off to visit his family in his native village of Panjao, in the Bamiyan region. He drove there very early in the morning of July 20, 2017, with his wife and two little boys. Late in the afternoon, while I was having a cup of tea with my friend Christine, my little "pocket pastor," who had arrived that very morning to see me again, I received a message from Saber telling me that he was at the Bamiyan Pelican School. With my agreement, he borrowed the Pelican 4x4 vehicle that was better equipped than his compact car to cross the mountains.

Christine and I spent a pleasant weekend together, telling each other about our lives and our projects while feasting on good cheeses and French sausages brought in her luggage.

Saturday morning, as the students entered the yard, Jawed, the night guard abruptly interrupted my conversation with a teacher to say the words that plunged us all into utter disarray: "Saber's been kidnapped!"

In shock, I leaned against the wall, hoping I had somehow misunderstood.

On Friday night, six armed guys had burst into the isolated house, tying up his family and beating them with sticks; then they took Saber away!

Panicked and stunned by this story, I called Bill, Nancy's husband, who happened to be in Kabul. His experience, his friendship, and his wisdom would be of great help. Moreover, a few days before, by chance, I had met the second adviser responsible for security at the French Embassy! I immediately decided to gather the employees of the Pelican to give them the news and assure them that the schools would remain open until further notice.

Everything happened very quickly. Gossip and rumors about the kidnapping were broadcast on the Bamiyan radio and posted on social networks, and I no longer knew who to believe or what to think. The first ransom demand was for $30,000. Then it jumped to $40,000 and then to $60,000. Finally, it stabilized at the initial figure corresponding more to the reality of Saber's financial situation. Indeed, professional kidnappers assess the amount of their potential victim's ransom by observing their lifestyle and researching their income. In Afghanistan, kidnappings have become big business and there are more than a hundred Afghans kidnapped every month. Due to this fact, prudent families set money aside to deal with this eventuality as quickly as possible.

I heard all sorts of rumors, some of which were defamatory and broke my heart, sowing seeds of doubt and suspicion about my colleague of almost seven years: "Saber robbed the NGO and pretends to be a victim; he faked his kidnapping and will leave for Europe with the ransom money." But I found out the group that had perpetrated the crime and claimed responsibility for it fed the Taliban's coffers. Negotiations with the family had begun and they were proving difficult. All the information we received was sent to my contact at the French Embassy, whom I called several times a day. I listened very carefully to this specialist in kidnappings and scrupulously followed his advice not to interfere in the case and to categorically refuse all contact with the thugs.

Two days after the kidnapping, local police caught one of the attackers who looked like Youssef, the former employee with a gun. I couldn't believe any of this, but how could I know for sure? The school's activities continued as normally as possible and the bakery kept up its production with Habibullah and Mortar, our two young bakers. Pastries and baguettes continued to be delivered throughout Kabul

I anticipated Monday, July 24th, with dread, as the pressure mounted. And after I got a phone call bluntly demanding that I pay the ransom, I realized I was becoming the kidnappers' next target. Strangers knocked on the school gate the next day, but the guard wouldn't let them in, and I refused to see them. After three attempts, they finally left. So with fear knotting my stomach, I decided not to spend the night at the center. Christine and I would go to the Serena Hotel, and I let the Embassy know.

Hearing about the latest events, the counselor asked me to calm down and wait for about twenty minutes. Then calling me back fifteen minutes later, he informed me that two armored cars with four French RAID policemen would come to get us after the children had left school. He also asked me not to go outside in the street and to gather my things without a suitcase so as not to arouse suspicion. Christine, more relaxed than me, joked around as usual. For my part, I gathered my plane ticket, my passport, some cash, and various official papers of the Pelican. Around 5:00 p.m., at the change of guards, I saw the day guard reluctantly leaving his post; the night guard whom I suspected of working with the kidnappers would take his place. Indeed, since the day before, that night guard had aggressively insisted that I pay the ransom since I was a signatory for the NGO. I learned later that he was Saber's brother-in-law.

Around 5:30 pm, I finally got a call from the RAID guys. Calling from the end of our street, they said they could see our yellow gate and were coming slowly toward us. But the infamous guard ignored my order to open the gate and went back into his hut, the telephone to his ear. Then as I grabbed the two-doored gate and opened it wide, I heard Jawed whisper in Dari: "*Pessa na meta, tchi kar mékonèm?*" "She won't give the money, what do we do?"

Not listening to the rest, I jumped into the first car and Christine into the second: our kidnapping wouldn't have lasted two minutes! We drove through Kabul and arrived an hour later at the *green zone* "campus" where the diplomats and other people from the various embassies lived in an ultra-secure location. We had two bedrooms and a bathroom there. The police were extremely attentive to us, and one even invited us to share a farewell drink. We really appreciated the comfort of a shower, a good dinner, and safe shelter, and in this protected setting, Christine and I managed to sleep quite peacefully.

The next day, Wednesday, July 26th at 8:00 a.m., I destroyed sensitive files, such as the Mossa case, and a Bible in Dari, in the shredder. I feared that watching me disappear would have them denounce me as a proselytizer, since I represented $200,000 in ransom for my kidnapping! We left for the airport in a car with diplomatic license plates and thankfully passed through the various controls without difficulty.

At 4:30 p.m. the plane took off and we landed in Dubai two and a half hours later. Christine, "delighted with her vacation" in Kabul, found a flight to Canton, since she was to leave for China on August 1. As for me, I took a flight to Paris where I landed the next day to catch the first train to Colmar. I was exhausted!

The first email from Kabul, from Nasima, arrived on Saturday, July 29: "Dear Ariane, I hope you are healthy and safe. You haven't been here for four days. It's hard to make the project work without you." This message would be followed by a few others showing me a lot of affection and asking me to come back as soon as possible.

I truly believe that God sent the angel Bill to counsel me, calm me down, and help me make the right decisions. My friend Christine with her humor and kindness symbolized the second angel, which came at just the right time! Moreover, the efficiency and wise advice of the French Embassy finally got us out of this trap.

After eleven days, Saber was released after his family paid the ransom, just a week after my hasty departure from Kabul. As my embassy contact wrote to me, "You made the right decision, Ariane, and you escaped being kidnapped."

I stayed in France for four months and administered the NGO with the help of an accounting firm whose director, a Christian from America, that I knew. It was necessary to continue to submit reports to the various Afghan Ministries and also to pay the last salaries since the project had been stopped. Despite everything, looking forward to my return and the resumption of Pelican activities, I kept on a few employees to serve as my contacts in Kabul and to ensure that the schools were not vandalized. I fumed with impatience more every day, never accepting the idea that our aid to the Hazaras was over. The Pelican had certainly been seriously injured, but the beautiful bird, I was sure, would heal its wounds, grow stronger, and get back on its feet. Then, ready to resume its course, it would open its wings wide and set off for the Afghan sky—God was not abandoning that country!

Chapter Forty-Three

Ariane's Thread

T he beautifully decorated streets of Colmar, close friends, my family, and the enticing menu of the Christmas dinner could not keep me from going back to Kabul to celebrate the birth of Jesus. So I left on December 10th and found the Afghan capital even worse than when I had left. Huge walls like the ramparts of fortified castles surrounded the buildings with watchtowers and armed guards. Checkpoints, barbed wire, military, police, and the wail of sirens invaded every neighborhood. One could not forget that this country was at war. All this violence contrasted surprisingly with the sweetness and kindness of Nasima, who, with roses in hand, greeted me at the airport. Farouk, also very moved, shook my hand for a long time and took my suitcase, wishing me: "Khosh Amédé, Ariane!" (Welcome, Ariane!) Then as the car started to take me back to the Pelican compound, he added quietly, "We didn't think you would come back."

So began two extremely difficult weeks as I got busy putting the project back on its feet. The faulty generator and the discharged batteries left me without any electricity as soon as the sun went down. The internet had been cut off, and one day the car even refused to start! But despite these burdensome worries, I never regretted my return.

On December 25th, while I was working in the office, planning the reopening of the schools, some of the Pelican employees arrived with gifts and my favorite Afghan dessert.

"Merry Christmas Ariane, we know it's a big celebration for you, and we came to tell you that the whole neighborhood was waiting for your return and that we can't wait to start school again."

My mouth full of sweet rice and pistachios, eyes clouded with emotion, I stammered, "Next week dear friends, I promise!"

There was no need for a formal announcement. The following Saturday at 6:00 a.m., the students crowded at our door and we all resumed our routine. The Pelican's wound had been attended to and healed, and the soaring bird had once again happily landed in Dasht e Barchi!

A few days later, I finally put my dream of creating a school, especially for the deaf, into action. The five classrooms, including a kindergarten, welcomed deaf students, boys and girls from three to forty-two years old. The sign language classes were given by six deaf teachers, four of whom were former students of Le Pélican! These deaf students joyfully joined the other students for meals, sports, and all kinds of fun activities.

Currently, more than eighty deaf people come to our school every day. So even if the terrorist attacks multiply and ISIS declares its intention to eradicate the Hazaras; even if the explosions arrive in our neighborhood, which is the most targeted; even if I am in danger with my Hazara friends, since it is God who prompted me to do more for the deaf, I will expand their school and with His strength, I will create other schools.

★★★

When I meditate on life, I recognize its difficulties, the harshness, and sometimes its tragedy. It seems to me that it cannot fully satisfy us if we do not believe in its extension *elsewhere*. We know we will not come out of it alive! Since the fall, we have been condemned to death from birth. Throughout our chaotic lives, we accept loopholes, I would even call it palliative care--the pleasures given by money, sex, power, and the various ways of hiding the question crucial to the meaning of life. I let myself be lulled by the disillusioned gaze of nihilistic authors for years. I totally adhered to certain philosophies affirming the absurdity of life, the illogical nature of morality, and the impossibility of finding the truth.

As a young woman, full of intellectual curiosity, I discovered Sartre, Nietzsche, and other thinker-philosophers who confirmed my theories of a world without God. Without wanting to denigrate these writers, I think I fell into the trap of my personal gullibility and arrogance. My dismissive attitude towards Christian authors led me to listen to the beguiling voices flattering my ego. Seduced by radical atheism and living without faith or law was so accommodating.

I regret that I didn't take the time or trouble to study and compare the various philosophies instead of accepting everything as a whole and playing the intellectual. What a mockery! The annihilation of any sense of life led, without my knowing it, to my personal ruin. I understood it much later, and I then grasped even more clearly the extraordinary gift of the Grace of God.

At the time of my little boy's tragic death, everything indeed fell apart. No philosophy provided a coherent answer to the subject of death and the meaning of life. In this gap arose the idea that I had to seek the truth, and I accepted the spiritual approach suggested by Jacques, as a last step before my leap into the void.

Today, reconciled with God and myself, I have found the truth. I believe that Jesus is the only one to embody it, and I am convinced that there is no other. So even if the pain of the deaths of Frantz and Jacques is not relieved, the wound is nevertheless mitigated by the assurance of a future reunion.

My mundane story represents nothing in the face of the misfortunes of the human race. I am a mother dispossessed of her child and a wife deprived of her husband; it is nothing exceptional. There are millions of others like me in the world. But I think that my story, as ordinary as it is, can become important, unique, and even valuable if it fits into the great history of humanity and its Creator.

After years of meditating deeply on the Scriptures, I understand that this book tells of the strange divine conspiracy, proposing the most extravagant plan of salvation, which the Bible itself tells us is considered by many to be foolish: "*For the message of the cross is foolishness to those who are perishing, but to us who are being saved, it is the power of God.*" (I Corinthians 1:18)

This unique God is One and Indivisible, united in three persons. Through the Son's incarnation and the working of the Holy Spirit, he revealed himself to humanity. This God, animated by infinite and eternal love, decided to save us. At Golgotha, Jesus, the Christ, agonizing in unspeakable suffering, reconciled us to God, the Father, and it was there that heaven and earth finally came together.

So, by this priceless gift, my story joins that of billions of others, to become, too, a jewel in the hand of God.

Yet, I know that if I had not made the effort to search the Scriptures, if I had refused to be touched by the Spirit introducing me to the divine perspective, and if finally, I had not accepted the Grace of God, life would have remained meaningless and mine would not have been worth living. The atheist existential writers would have gotten the better of me, and I would no doubt have taken my life.

How could I have found meaning in the death of my ten-year-old son? How could I find an explanation for the death of Jacques, who was brilliantly leading humanitarian work in the name of the Lord?

Our lives only have meaning if they are integrated into the plan of God, who, madly in love with his creatures, wants them to be with him for eternity. Circumstances, happy or unhappy, will not change the Lord's plan to bring us back to paradise lost.

And if I give meaning to life, then I become able to give meaning to death.

I know that the Bible does not contain a magic formula to save us from suffering. On the contrary, it reveals to us the reality that this world is in spiritual ruin as a consequence of rebellion against God. On the other hand, I also understand that it invites us to discover the mercy of God and his plan of salvation for all of us.

It has been my freedom, my gift, and my most beautiful choice for more than thirty years.

Chapter Forty-Four

EPILOGUE

W riting this book was a painful process, and for some who have experienced or witnessed similar traumas, it may be painful to read. It could bring back long-buried suffering. But I wanted to tell my story, knowing that the experiences of others can sometimes help one move in the right direction.

Revisiting these memories opened up unhealed wounds again and immense pain, like undergoing an operation with no anesthesia, often overwhelmed me.

When I was deeply discouraged, my other self, Jacques, would come along with me into this bitter past. He knew how to quell my anxiety, sweep away my doubts, and help me relive those six months when we powerlessly watched our child die.

All these moments, awash in tears, torn with revulsion, and invaded by the darkest sorrow, dragged us back into the horror, and yet we remained confident in our belief in God, and found a way out of our despair. We were filled with a confidence that God had placed at our disposal without the limits of time or circumstance. It is that confidence of which the prophet speaks: *"In repentance and rest is your salvation, in quietness and trust is your strength."* (Isaiah 30:15)

This immersion into the past is neither self-pity nor navel-gazing. Yet, "one does not write in the first person singular with impunity," says the writer Frédéric Beigbeder.

Psychologists would probably say that I wrote this book to exorcise moments so painful that my heart could no longer contain them. But that was never the case—the narrative rekindled far too much grief. I understand today that words have been my allies, and that they have fulfilled a soothing function.

These pages have no other purpose than to reveal the overwhelming goodness of God, his infinite grace, and the paths he has taken to meet us. Believers will have no trouble recognizing the little touches of grace and the miracles, the providential encounters and all those scattered pieces of the puzzle that were put together according to a divine plan.

And this story of our little boy, who died of leukemia, is one of the 1,600 cases of children diagnosed with different kinds of cancer each year in France. Children are dying of disease, abuse, hunger, and war all over the world. Frantz joined the cohort of unfinished young lives, and our suffering was, like that of other parents, commensurate with our love for our child—unfathomable.

Through this book, I would also like to give some guidance to those who, faced with the shock of the death of a loved one's child, do not know how to react to the distress of the parents. Because in this ordeal, good intentions are not enough. Compassion, friendship, and love make it possible to find ways to support and accompany parents living this drama. You still have to know how to follow these paths on tiptoe and admit the possibility of making mistakes and being rebuffed, without ever being discouraged.

I also wrote this book at the request of close friends who believed an account of our journey would be valuable for other people in pain. And I finished the book without Jacques to keep my promise to explain how and by whom our lives were transformed.

I sought God, gropingly, with rage and a lost heart, determined to find him or die.

Finally, like the blind man of Siloam, I saw the Light and never let it go again.

So, not to testify would have been cowardice and laziness, ingratitude and indifference.

If I could help those in darkness, if my story could truly encourage those who are hopeless and move them to look beyond their doubts and rebellion, then writing this book will not have been in vain.

For my part, I decided to enter fully into God's plan. I don't wonder why these tragedies happened to me, because the most terrible suffering can lead to a new path of life, and I wonder, rather, what I will do with it. I can choose to let myself sink or to cross the trials by surpassing myself. "You can become bitter or better," is a phrase that has always guided me.

Finally, I wanted to write here that an unhappy fate can point to what is truly important, and that, through suffering, we can find God and grow, because it expands our hearts and opens us to other perspectives. From that point on, we are no longer victims bent under the weight of an obscure fatalism, but simply wounded people able to accept the new life offered.

Encouraged by the extraordinary news of Easter morning, I choose not to let my pain be a curtain of tears preventing me from seeing the light. I now accept death without struggle because I believe in future reunions.

"He will wipe every tear from their eyes. There will be no more death or mourning or crying or pain, for the old order of things has passed away." (Revelation 21:4)

Only the Lord knows the answer, and only he knows what I am still capable of accomplishing for his glory and how to maintain my fragile balance during my last years on this earth.

Sometimes, under the starry skies of Afghan nights, I dream of chapter seven of Revelation. I imagine God descending majestically from his throne; He walks through the crowd and stops to wipe the tears from each face. Then he says with utmost gentleness: "Don't cry anymore, Ariane, it's over, all is well. I invite you to the joyous celebrations of the ultimate victory over death. Come celebrate with us the abundant life that my Son has given you…"

So I look forward to rediscovering my original innocence, and with Jacques and Frantz at my side, peacefully await the moment when, as in the new Garden of Eden, the Lord God will once again visit his children.

Lord, I want to give you all the glory that is due to you.

I want to reveal your Love and your Mercy.
Tell your wonders.
Add nothing, omit nothing.
Simply tell the events as they happened.
To speak of the eruption of grace and the dazzling presence
of God in the chaos of my life.
To tell how you lifted me from darkness
and transported me into the dazzling Light.
To tell you, finally, of my adoration and my gratitude.

www.ingramcontent.com/pod-product-compliance
Lightning Source LLC
Chambersburg PA
CBHW071150130626

46553CB00004B/1593